Escaping The Fear

My Story Of Survival

Lynne Hanson

**chipmunkapublishing
the mental health publisher**

All rights reserved, no part of this publication may be reproduced by any means, electronic, mechanical photocopying, documentary, film or in any other format without prior written permission of the publisher.

Published by
Chipmunkapublishing
PO Box 6872
Brentwood
Essex CM13 1ZT
United Kingdom

http://www.chipmunkapublishing.com

Copyright © Lynne Hanson 2012

Edited by Sandra Nimako - Boatey

ISBN   978-1-84991-864-0

Chipmunkapublishing gratefully acknowledge the support of Arts Council England.

Acknowledgements

I would not be here today, nor to have written this book, if it had not been for the following people. I owe them my life and I am deeply grateful for all the help and support they gave me during a very difficult time.

In the UK:- I thank my local G.P., my health visitor, Diane, and my Domestic Violence support worker, Sharon, for helping me leave my ex-husband.

I thank the local church – especially Mabel and Tim and Yvonne, who were always there for me.

I thank Becky for helping me through the Cognitive Behavioural Therapy.

In Spain:- I thank Fr G. Johnston for reading through the first draft of this book and offering suggestions to improve the wording and our friend Bill, who also read this manuscript and advised me on legal matters.

I would also like to thank all my friends and family who have supported me, especially my husband, Ian, for believing in me and being so supportive.

Finally, I would like to express my gratitude to the team at Chipmunka Publishing for bringing this book into the public domain.

Escaping The Fear

Introduction

I am writing this book so that my family and friends may understand how I have come to be the person they now know. My story also highlights many shortcomings in the legal, health, social services, police and benefit systems.

This will be an honest and open account and therefore bound to be upsetting at times.

I explain how for most of my life I have lived in fear – as a child because of my mother, at school because I was scared to answer questions in case I was wrong, at work because I might not have been good enough and then the devastating 11 years with my ex-husband, (whom I shall refer to as Henry), during which time I almost lost my life. His quest for power and control is unbelievable – as is his credibility.

A lot of the issues I have had to deal with concerned my mother; now that my father is no longer with us, I feel that I can put my feelings in writing so as not to cause him any further distress.

I will attempt to write this chronologically – I find that makes more sense to people reading it – and it is also easier for me to write it that way.

I also hope that this book will show other people who have endured any form of domestic violence that there is a way out. The authorities (globally) must learn to understand that no person in that situation is 'low risk'. There have been far too many women killed by their husband, partner or ex. A few years ago there was a news item about a domestic abuse case in Spain – the judge decreed that as the woman was so well dressed she could not possibly have been the victim of domestic violence! I was outraged. It was fortunate that I was seeing a women's support group that morning, as I was so angry. What planet do these judges live on? We all have free will (God given) and are therefore able to chose how we dress.

Spain has since worked hard to overcome those attitudes but still even now, June 2012, the papers report that 620 women suffer some sort of domestic abuse every week. A much lower number of men also suffer – the exact number is difficult to determine, as men are much more reluctant to come forward and admit what is happening to them. Sadly there are still reports every week of people being killed by their partner. This is totally unacceptable. It is also insulting to be told by police that 'you don't know what you are talking about'. Any complaint of this nature must be taken seriously.

Many women living in an abusive relationship often end up on psychiatric wards, this is definitely not the correct 'treatment' for abuse and adds to the trauma even more. It seems to me that many psychiatrists only want to give people drugs to keep them quiet – they should listen to their nursing staff; one very good psychiatric nurse obviously understood that there was more to my situation than I had let on, and that in her opinion psychiatrists are 'treating' the wrong partner!

Having then been given a history of psychiatric hospital admissions, any complaint of domestic violence is dismissed by the police and social services as nonsense; I can still hear the scorn in the policeman's voice when he said that I did not know what I was saying or doing because I was mentally ill. Police and social services are meant to be there to protect people, not to make a diagnosis.

That attitude HAS to change.

What I was suffering from, along with most other women in my situation was 'mental distress'; there is a big difference between mental distress and mental illness and mental health doctors need to recognise that fact. I still have a great deal of distress as I have not seen my youngest son and daughter for over 7 years now. Any mother will tell you - 'that hurts'.

Escaping The Fear

Earliest Memories

I was born in Barrow-in-Furness, which in 1954 was still in Lancashire; my mother, Joan, was not married to my biological father. That was not the done thing at the time and I thought that she was either brave or awkward in keeping me. I later discovered that neither of those opinions were correct. I weighed 4lbs 2oz at birth, was in an incubator and baptised in the nearest catholic church, (St Mary's in Duke Street on 11th July 1954) – this knowledge came to me just over 50 years later! Apparently Joan was living with my biological father in some rather awful tenements that were pulled down in 1956. The story is that Joan had left me with my father whilst she was out (at work I presume), she returned to find the babysitter and my father somewhat entangled, and being of a violent nature, she stabbed him. (She did what a lot of people had wanted to do to people who annoyed them– maybe she was being more honest than the rest of us who do not admit to having those sort of feelings.) However, courts do not look favourably on that sort of behaviour and I have been told that Joan served 6 months in prison. So where was I? - As I later found out, I was in foster care whilst Joan was serving her time.

The only father I knew was Ron, he adopted me in May 1960 – which is why my birth certificate was dated 1960. I knew that I was different in my mother's eyes because of her treatment towards me. I assumed it was because having me had stopped her working – she was a crane-driver at Vicker's shipyard during the day and a nightclub singer in the evenings. She was a strong, independent woman who could solve cryptic crosswords in The Times! She was also a very angry and violent person. I remember that she used to have lovely auburn hair which, for some unknown reason, she later dyed black.

Ron met Joan in 1957 (according to my brother), which meant that I was three years old. Ron was in the Royal Marines and sent to Barrow for some reason. He met Joan at a night club where she was singing. Ron then left his wife, Joyce and his son Roderick; when we lived in Portsmouth we were only two roads away from them. Roderick would often ride his bike past where we lived in the hope that he would see his dad – Ron. Ron never really had anything to do with Roderick until Roderick's daughter made contact about 16 years ago. My brother thinks that this had quite a negative effect on Roderick – he and his family now live in New Zealand.

Joan was the second eldest of 11 children. Her father was an alcoholic, so most of the money ended up in the local pub. He was apparently quite aggressive and Joan would take money out of his pockets and give it to her mum when he had passed out from too much alcohol.

I have no memories at all of living in Barrow. My earliest memories are vague to say the least; I remember a dressing up box in the house in Festing Grove, Portsmouth and having an invisible (to everyone but me) friend called Sally. She would come out of the wall to play with me, had a place at the dinner table and a seat in the car. My father had a black car and the journey up to Barrow seemed to take forever; no sooner had we reached the end of our road, I would be asking, "Are we there yet?" and usually be sick several times on the journey.

I know that I must have been in Portsmouth in November 1959, (I would have been 5 years old), because I have the photograph that Ron took of me at the periscope on a submarine, it was called 'Midget Submariner' and with the sailor's hat, my curls and my cheeky grin, I am sure that he won a competition with it.

I always thought that my brother, John, was 5 years younger than me, I was wrong, he is 4 years younger than me, and Joan and Ron didn't marry until May 1960, (they were waiting for Ron's divorce from Joyce). I have no idea when Joan, Ron and I moved down to Portsmouth and John tells me that he was born in Arundel (35 Kings Road) in Sussex.

From Portsmouth, we all moved to Lagos, which was then the capital of Nigeria. I remember John trying to ride his tricycle down the stone steps in our house there and the houseboy, Ouadoo (probably not spelt like that) with his many wives. I remember attending the local school which was a two room hut, where the teacher only spoke French before moving on to a bigger school where I took a day off as I had misheard the teacher's instructions! I have vague memories of seeing hippo's in rivers, but couldn't say if that was while living in Nigeria or Northern Rhodesia.

I think we stayed in Lagos for about a year before returning to the UK; we may have lived somewhere near Caterham, Surrey, but I am not really sure. We lived in an old unused shop in Caterham just down the road from Grandma. The shop windows were whitewashed. We had a small garden at the back of the house and on Sundays we would go to church at the Army barracks and Sunday school. John remembers one of Ron and Joan's arguments when she locked him out of the house. It was during this time back in the UK that my sister Rowena was born and I still have the letter I wrote to Joan after Rowena's birth. John and I were placed in foster homes a couple of times and the people were awful to me; they loved John – he was a cute little 3 year old and I was just a nuisance. The foster home was in Thames Ditton – it was terrible and John has now told me that he was always being hit by their son who was bigger than him – it was a very unpleasant time for both of us.

We sailed back to Africa sometime around 1963, (the liners outward /return were called Union Castle and Pretoria Castle). We lived in Ndola, the capital of Northern Rhodesia where John and I attended a convent school. I have a few memories of my time at that school – I thought that as all the schoolboys had to go to another school when they reached a certain age (10, I think), that the nuns ate little boys and I was so worried about John. The head mistress was called sister De Laselles – John's teacher was called Sister Albatina. My main teacher was the lady who lived opposite us. The nuns were really quite cruel; I can remember being hit over my knuckles with a ruler for playing wrong notes when sight reading during my piano lessons. It was a long walk home from school for me on my own, I was a day student – it was a boarding school. John and I were driven to school each morning by Amos (he was sacked by Joan for drawing on one of my dolls). The school day began at 8am and finished at 2pm – it was too hot to study in the afternoon, even for the nuns in their white habits. Once back home I would generally have a swim in the pool – after the water scorpions and turtles had been scooped out!

I remember Joan smiling whilst we lived there – I don't think that ever happened after we returned to the UK.

I have a few memories about food; waiting for my bowl of chilli to cool down, some dessert called 'fridge cake' – made with a base of 'Nice' biscuits and curries being placed in the middle of a ring of rice on your plate and then you added the extras you wanted, e.g., peanuts, coconut, pineapple, raisins, etc. I can't remember them all and I can't recall the name of the dish.

My youngest sister, Fiona, was born while we lived in Ndola; when she was very little she would ask "If I was born in Africa, why aren't I black?"

The bungalow was huge – as I remember it – and was set in the middle of an acre of land; 2 large lawns (1 at the front and 1 at the back), a large rose garden, a kidney shaped swimming pool, a banana plantation and an orchard. Everyone had servants, so there was a houseboy, a cook, several gardeners and a nanny. I liked to sit with the servants around the fire they lit in the gardens and eat meelies (sweetcorn) with them that they had roasted on the fire – I was always in trouble for that!

I was in serious trouble one day when Joan put baby Fiona on the ground by the pool – Fiona rolled into the pool and I was severely punished for allowing that to happen. Sunday was the nanny's day off and that meant I was in charge of looking after my brother John, 4; my sister Rowena, 2, and the new baby, Fiona:- I was only 9 years old myself! Strange things used to happen to me there as well, I no-longer saw my 'invisible' friend Sally but at night all the dolls on the large trunk in my bedroom would come to life and dance!

I remember the journeys to and from Africa, the first time by plane there and back and the last time by boat, on that last journey I used to play chess with a man, he also taught me to play "I Wanna Hold Your Hand" on the piano. The boat went through The Suez Canal and I saw a 'Camel Train'; I have to admit that I was most disappointed that the camels were not actually pulling a train! There was a lot of food – it always seemed to be a mealtime and the scrambled egg was awful – it sloshed all over the plate and Joan made me eat it all – then I was sick. I must have contracted a bladder infection on the journey as I started having to go the toilet every few minutes; as soon as I got back to my cabin I needed to go again. That also got me in trouble with Joan, she could see me leave the cabin and walk to the toilet, so I had to find another route!

Early Education

My early education was very disrupted due to the frequent moves and I think I went to 13 different infant and junior schools before becoming settled at Pendleton High School for Girls in Salford. We arrived back in the UK just in time for me to sit the 11 plus exam, so that would be 1963 or 1964. I came 'borderline' in that exam and had to sit another set of exams which I passed.

I have never understood how or why Ron and Joan chose a house in Park Road, Salford; it was a large house just on the border of Eccles and very near Hope Hospital. It was big, old and very scary. Ron was working at Granada film studios as a film cameraman and drove into work so I'm sure we could have lived somewhere nicer. Because of the nature of Ron's work I met some 'interesting' characters:- Charles Haughtrey stands out because he used to like visiting our house to play with our dolls house and tea set! Ron told me about the time he was filming at Margaret Rutherford's house – he needed the bathroom and when he put the toilet seat up, written around the edge were the words – 'Hurrah! There's a man in the house!' Ron would also tell us about how he would film rides at Blackpool whilst being strapped to the outside of the roller coaster and hang upside down from helicopters. I'm sure he preferred that, to being shot down whilst parachuting. He was a war hero and a very courageous man. I can never understand how such a man could be so afraid of my mother.

This is probably not unique but, I actually dreaded the school holidays. Joan had got used to having servants around and that meant that I became those servants - skirting boards were a major issue, being inspected daily! I dreaded being sent out to get the shopping as Joan would scrutinise the receipts, and count the change, if there was any discrepancy I was either sent back to sort it out or I would make it up out of the pocket money Ron gave me.

Every day was filled with fear:- what have I missed, what should I have done, was the ironing done to Joan's standards, were the clothes put away correctly? Of course everything I did was wrong; "Your head will never save your legs!" was a frequent put down, if I didn't carry enough crockery from the kitchen to the cupboard in the morning room; the ironing was neither "done nor left alone". It was my job to wash up, look after John and my sisters, clean the house and I still had school work to get through.

When I got home from school I had to look after my siblings, set the table ready for tea and on no account was I to play with anyone. I did that one afternoon and was in serious trouble because I hadn't set the table! After tea I had to wash the pots and then set the table in the morning room ready for breakfast next day. Of course I still had my homework to get through and by the time that was finished I was shattered.

Another task was to take the dog for a walk (when we had one); Joan must have liked large dogs and I can remember Brutus a Great Dane, and Hassan an Afghan Hound; I am not sure which was first though. The dogs in Ndola were Brumus (Collie) and Chummy (Boxer). Chummy 'disappeared' one day and I think he was taken by some other servants to feed their families.

My way of coping in my mind was music. I had piano lessons with an elderly bachelor not far away. My friend Beverley, who lived in the same street, also had lessons with him. We used to try to arrange it that she would arrive just before my lesson finished as he used to like to brush my hair (which was long then) and he gave me the creeps. When I was in my later teens I was allowed out on a Sunday with my friend Jane to go to the Opus One concerts by the Hallé Orchestra at the Free Trade Hall in Manchester.

Joan had decided for some strange reason that I was to be a doctor – that was certainly NOT my intention, I enjoyed music and was good at the subject. So in an act of defiance when Mrs Cohen (music teacher) came into the physics lab one day and asked if anyone was interested in doing music 'O' level, I put my name down at once and gave up History and Geography. I paid for that when Joan found out but I felt that I had gained a slight victory. Joan's revenge was to stop my piano lessons but I still took it in turns with Jane to come top in the music exams! I also took violin lessons for a while but I kept leaving my violin on the bus. Joan would not be happy with me about that and so one day when I had left the wretched instrument on the bus going to school, I was in a big panic; I was frightened to tell Joan. I sneaked out of school at lunchtime and walked over to Frederick Road Bus Station to collect it, they wanted five shillings and sixpence for it! I had no money on me and so had to confess to Joan; she phoned the Bus Depot and told them "You can bloody well keep the thing!" Thus ended my violin career. I gained "O" levels in English Language, English Literature, French, Mathematics, Physics, Chemistry and Music; I failed Latin and was devastated – I didn't fail exams – I didn't dare!

Moving into the sixth form was a nightmare; I wanted to study music and English literature, but Joan was still insistent I should study medicine. This presented a big problem as it was necessary to have three sciences at "A" level; I had physics and chemistry at "O" level but not biology. The (disastrous) solution to that dilemma was that I had to study biology "O" level every lunch hour. I had a Saturday job (Woolworth's at St Mary's Gate in Manchester until it closed down) and then, along with most of the sixth form, at the new Mark's and Spencer's at Salford Precinct. I also still had the housework and care of my siblings. My physics teacher, Miss Ross, commented on one of my reports that "my behaviour in class suggested that I was either permanently tired or bored". Guess which it was, I was shattered. Three hours of homework each night plus the extra biology study, housework, shopping, trying to keep John, Rowena and Fiona safe from Joan's violent outbursts and also trying to protect them from the terrible fights between Joan and Ron.

Another big and terrifying problem was the house itself. All of us children were scared to be alone in it, or go up the stairs at night alone; there were many scary, unexplainable incidents – that could be another book! I would see 'shadows' of figures moving around. I would see images in the mirror in my bedroom, but one of the scariest incidents was when we were all in bed – Joan and Ron were out as usual – I was feeling quite unsettled when suddenly I heard a thudding noise moving across the ceiling. I lay in bed totally still and held my breath. The noise then moved down the wall and as it got to just above my head I screamed out, dashed to the wall and put the light on; there was nothing to be seen. John came in to my room and I accused him of trying to frighten me – he did like playing tricks but it was unfair of me to blame John. I am sure that he understands it was better for me to think that the noise had a 'human' origin, rather than let my imagination get carried away.

Joan's 'Bibles' were:- 'The Encyclopaedia of Witchcraft and Demonology' and 'Magic and the Supernatural'. These books were lying around for us to see and being inquisitive children we couldn't help but look at them – the pictures in them really scared me and I am sure they must have had the same effect on my siblings. She also used a 'ouiji' board, so did she really 'summon' up some evil spirits? Was there something already in the house? Or was it just Joan's personality and the fact of having four young children?

Joan was not at all happy when we came back to England. One issue was that she resented the fact that her Rhodesian driving licence was not valid in the UK. That problem could have been easily rectified but she absolutely refused to take another driving test, so I had no sympathy with her. She also missed having all the servants – now she was down to one – me. Joan and I rarely did anything together, she never taught me how to cook or bake but she did make sure that I could sew as she wanted me to shorten all of her dresses. I dreaded Saturday mornings as Ron and Joan would go off to do the 'big shop' and I would be left in charge of the little ones and they would always play up! That problem resolved itself when I got to the sixth form and took a Saturday job.

Joan's situation improved when she started working as ASM (Assistant Stage Manager – a glorified prompt!) on Coronation Street. She and Pat Phoenix (Elsie Tanner) became great drinking buddies and I can remember being turfed out of my bed on several occasions as Pat was 'too tired' to go home! One afternoon Sandra Gough (who played the daughter of Stan and Hilda Ogden) took me to see "The Sound of Music" at the cinema. It is a very long film and when I got home Joan asked how many times had I watched it? She was very unpleasant and would not believe how long the film actually was.

An awful incident occurred one Friday afternoon, it must have been during some school holidays, Ron and Joan were both at work and I was in charge. Rowena and Fiona were playing in their bedroom and I was in the lounge downstairs, suddenly I saw a body come flying past the window outside – it was Fiona! She said Rowena wouldn't stop following her so she jumped out of the window; she later claimed that it was a bet over 3 felt-tip pens! So, a visit to casualty at Hope Hospital and more trouble for me.

We would spend many summers in Barrow visiting Nana and I would often stay with Uncle Ken, Auntie Alice and their daughter Judith. She was just a little younger than me and we got on well together. I am the eldest of all the grandchildren, and therefore had to look after any of my cousins who also visited. I remember one afternoon taking my brother and sisters and several cousins to the big park near where Nana lived, but I 'lost' Rowena. She was eventually 'found' by someone who knew our family and they brought her back home safe and sound. I was not in Joan's good books, once again.

I also got on well with Aunty Chris – she was 5 years older than me and she would give me her cast off dresses. Because Chris and I were close, if I told Joan that I didn't like something that Chris didn't like also, she would say that I was only copying Chris and that I should get a mind of my own. Joan only once told me that she loved me, but that was after she had drunk her bottle of sherry!

When I was about 14 I ran away from home, Joan and Ron were out; I made sure the children were all asleep and left the house with just a little bag. I had no idea where I was going or what I would do, I just wanted to get away; the police picked me up very late at night/early morning and phoned Ron. He came out to collect me and never said a word. Back at the house Joan gave me a slap and asked "What if anything had happened to the little ones?" It didn't matter to her that something might have happened to me – my feelings were confirmed – she hated me and had no regard for my safety or quality of life. She and Ron still went out the next night though as that was a Saturday and Mrs Brizland always babysat on Saturdays! When I went to kiss Joan goodnight, she turned her face away.

So why did I run away away? A couple of days beforehand Joan was telling me about one of my Aunts who had been adopted, she then added, "Oh, and by the way, so are you!" All she would say was that she was my mother but Ron was not my father. I was totally devastated, Ron and I were very close; neither Ron or Joan would talk to me about it, Ron just said that I didn't need to know anything. I didn't know how to handle the situation , so I left.

Horror of horrors, I failed all my "A" levels! Well actually, I was given "O" level grades in them which meant that I gained biology "O" level – so now I had eight "O" levels. I was actually very relieved at not getting any "A" levels. You see, on the UCCA form I managed to get the last entry down to dentistry (the first four were for medicine); I went for an interview at Manchester University and they offered me three 'E's! All I can assume is that they were desperate for dental students but I had no desire to be a dentist either! Joan was furious, "You failed those A levels on purpose!" I didn't, I worked as hard as I could, but it was all too much and I was at breaking point in the sixth form – it was only talking with my music teacher that helped me.

So what was I to do now? The thought of being at 'home' with Joan was not appealing so I found myself a job. First at a shoe shop in Manchester and then at the

Inland Revenue based in Highland House (close by Victoria bus station) – life got even worse. I also had an interview for "The Wrens" and had to go to Liverpool for that. I was not accepted and Joan was furious, it had been another of her ideas. She asked me if I had been questioned about my 'relationship' with my best friend, Jane, from school and then accused me of being a lesbian! I was extremely upset at this and so was Jane; Jane's mother 'phoned Joan and 'had words'. My friendship with Jane was not the same after that and we went our separate ways in life.

Joan got up at 10.30am in the week, I had to listen out for her getting up and have her coffee (made with hot milk) ready for her as soon as she came down – I was panic stricken every morning in case I got the timing wrong. The other tasks escalated – shopping, cleaning, ironing. One day she complained again that 'the ironing was neither done nor left alone', I had had enough and snapped – my reply was "Well bloody well do it yourself then" and I left the house. Now what do I do, I thought, but all I could do was return – she ignored me completely.

Further Education and Work

I gained a place at "The School of Radiography" in Barrow and went there after working at Highland House – that is where I met Chris, we later married and had a son – Paul. As soon as I left home my room was known as the 'spare room' – Joan was rid of me. It seemed to me then that I had no family back in Salford, my visits back were infrequent and I always felt 'in the way'. That meant that contact with John, Rowena and Fiona was all but lost. I was sure that they thought I had abandoned them and saved myself by getting out.

Things didn't quite work out for me in Barrow though. I had a room with an elderly widow called Mrs Kidd and I needed to go into hospital to have an ovarian cyst removed. While still in hospital Mrs Kidd told me that I must find somewhere else to live. Luckily, my Uncle Doug and his wife Sylvia let me stay with them. I spent ten days in hospital and three weeks at a convalescent home. Next, the school of radiography shut down and I transferred to Stockport to be near Chris; Joan then stopped my grant so I had to leave the course and find a job; that is how I ended up working for the county courts in Manchester first and then in Stockport at Heron House. It was during that time that Chris and I married.

Just before our wedding I was admitted to St Thomas' Hospital on a psychiatric ward and was given six treatments of ECT. Joan's behaviour towards me had really taken away my confidence or maybe I had none to be taken, everything I did had been ridiculed by her. I had written a short piece of music for my "O" level music assignment, Mrs Cohen's comment on it was 'Brilliant – just like Beethoven'. I was so proud of that and played the piece for Joan, she smirked and left the room.

Although psychiatrists insist that there are no side effects from ECT, I have to protest that they are wrong. Immediately afterwards there is the awful headache and then the memory loss. This can lead to all sorts of problems, in consultations with other medical staff they cannot believe that someone can 'forget' important details about their medical history and family background. They have blasted your brain without a clue as to what they are really doing and think it's not going to have any affect! It is surely time that this barbaric treatment is stopped and even banned.

Whilst working at The County Courts in Stockport I asked them to sponsor me on an Open University course – the Maths Foundation – they refused saying that I wasn't capable. That annoyed me somewhat, even though I only wanted to do the course because a man in a pub when I was out with Chris had said, "Women can't do maths!" I ignored the civil service and did the course anyway – the OU wouldn't let me on the summer school though as I was 9 months pregnant with Paul! I passed that course and took the Science Foundation Course. Unfortunately during that year Paul's father and I split up and after a few moves I found myself yet again in Portsmouth. Divorces are never nice things to go through but Chris and I did get to stage where we could talk to each other and he even came to my 50th birthday party. Looking back, I probably married him to try and escape from Joan and my past; that doesn't work and is not a good basis for a marriage.

While I was with Chris in our little cottage in Whaley Bridge there was some contact with my brother and sisters, but when I should have gone to Ron and Joan's house to deliver Easter Eggs I had to cancel, I was still frightened of Joan.

I moved down to Portsmouth with a friend called Arthur, (he died in the mid 90's), he was a contract draughtsman who worked abroad a lot. I agreed to move down with him. We let people assume that we were 'a couple', the truth is that he was impotent and had no interest in having an intimate relationship. I never told anyone about that as I did not want to embarrass him. While in Portsmouth, I learned that the OU were trying to get a Combined Sciences Degree off the ground at Bournemouth University. I applied but this didn't happen as there were not enough people applying. However, Arthur told me that there was a Polytechnic in Portsmouth, so I applied there. At my interview, I had baby Paul with me and he was emptying all the boxes in the room as Mr Howarth had just moved offices. I was offered a place on a Physics degree course! I agreed as I was picking up books that Paul had 'unpacked'. That is how you end up on a physics degree course!

Ron would often be in London on business, and we would meet up (without Joan knowing). She was very jealous of my relationship with Ron and I never understood why. Ron later explained the reason for this many years later, just before he died. I was in foster care when Ron met Joan and it was he who insisted that I live with them. That then explained a great deal – Joan hadn't wanted me at all and she made certain that I knew it.

Those years at Portsmouth Polytechnic were good. After my degree I went to Southampton University to gain a PGCE (Post Graduate Certificate) in maths and physics. I then taught Science at St. Anne's Convent School for a year and then returned to Portsmouth to do an M.Sc. in Microwave Solid State Physics. I moved up to Hayfield, in the Peak District, and continued my studies, which entailed going back to Portsmouth to take the exams;

my thesis was carried out at Manchester, UMIST, (University of Manchester Institute of science and Technology).

I worked at Lo Cost in Whaley Bridge on a temporary basis before getting a position as a lecturer at High Peak College – in Nutrition and Hygiene! That was only a temporary job. I started work at BNFL, (British Nuclear Fuels Limited) based at Risley July 1989 – first of all in Corporate Marketing – which wasn't my scene and then in Safety – which was! During that time I bought a house in Buxton, with Arthur; that proved to be a great mistake and I actually only stayed there for five weeks. There were many reasons for that decision but a main one was having to leave at 6am to get to work. I decided that I should leave Buxton and stayed in BNFL apartments at Risley. That meant that I couldn't have Paul with me and as he had only just entered the fourth form at school and was therefore starting his GCSE work, I didn't want to move him from his school – I knew how disruptive that had been for me. So, I spoke with Paul's dad and we arranged for Paul to live with him until I could find somewhere more appropriate to live; I honestly thought that it would just be a temporary arrangement. I had also seen a solicitor in Risley to arrange to get my name removed from the deeds of the Buxton house and I thought that had happened, a very costly mistake on my part.

It was while working at BNFL that I met up again with Henry whom I had known since leaving school as he had been in my ex-husband's circle of friends. We had common interests – music and walking – and he was a bit 'eccentric'.

We got together as in couple in 1990 and I moved into his house in the North of England. I spent one whole weekend tidying his front room and another washing all the crockery, cutlery, pots and pans, and another weekend sorting out his garden as he wanted to sell that house. His plan was for us to buy a house together, get married and have children – he wanted four! At that time I felt so proud and pleased that someone like him could possibly want to be with someone like me. One day Henry saw me reading 'Men are from Mars, Women are from Venus' and he became very angry with me, he confiscated the book and hid it! His reason was that 'I do not need to know about that'. Was that the first 'warning sign'?

Everything seemed to be fine then, he was eccentric but I didn't think he was dangerous. How wrong I was! I started to be unwell again; I was given more anti-depressants and saw a CPN (Community Psychiatric Nurse) a couple of times a week during my lunch hour.

One day Henry asked me to invigilate him in an exam – I agreed and asked what the subject was, it was astrology and I was surprised – he had kept that secret. He took me to a meeting at the local Spiritualist Church, it must have been around July 1992. It seemed to be just like a normal church service but instead of a sermon a guest speaker got up and gave messages to people in the 'congregation' from their deceased loved ones. That particular evening was taken by a lady and I was completely taken aback when she came to me; she said that my Grandad was with her, (all I can remember of him is being told off for cutting all the fat off any meat and for making sure that the cards were kept neat when I played clock patience – he taught that game to me). She also told me that she had a child in spirit with her who was my first baby (I had had a miscarriage before Paul), and that he was doing fine; her final piece of news was that I had another baby on the way. I was unaware that I was pregnant at that time, but a test the week after confirmed my condition and Ben (as I shall refer to him here) was on his way!

In fact I later concluded that Henry's faith in astrological charts and tarot card readings is a very good excuse for not having to accept personal responsibility for his behaviour and actions; he is free to do exactly what he wants, when he wants because it is fate. The perfect answer to irresponsibility!

My Life with Henry.

Henry wanted a bigger house and drew up a list of ten 'essentials' for our house and I was instructed to find it. Every house I found in his chosen area was rejected and I stupidly told him about a house I had seen for sale elsewhere. What a mistake that was! It was an old doctor's surgery and was massive – about 19 rooms and was on a main road. We viewed the house on several occasions and moved into it in 1992 when I was four months pregnant.

The house was owned by two gay men who had been together for 14 years; as they had now both retired they decided to move to their apartment in Malta. They were 'difficult' to deal with to say the least, but Henry was very persuasive.

The house was built as a doctor's house and surgery; that meant that it had two front doors – one being the patients' entrance that led into the waiting room, a hatchway connected that to the dispensary. Another door led off the waiting room to a small hallway and through to the surgery itself. Another door connected to the main huge L-shaped hall. The lounge and dining rooms were enormous and were separated by velvet curtains which had replaced the original folding wooden doors. There was a large kitchen and a very large laundry room with a toilet attached. The main stairway led to a bathroom, separate toilet and 5 bedrooms; a narrower stairway led up to the servants quarters in the attic – this was curtained off and was very creepy. The cellar was divided into three sections. I didn't like going down there either as it would flood during heavy rain and I would find dead mice floating on the water and frogs hopping about.

Henry took the 'master bedroom' with the fancy ceiling and he gave me the bedroom next door which had the en-suite shower, but no toilet; this had been a kitchen when part of the upstairs had been a separate flat. The shower was also en-suite to another large bedroom which Henry used as his 'library'. I wanted to decorate the smallest bedroom to use as a nursery – this never happened as he was too concerned with his library.

As the house was so big Henry agreed to buy quite a lot of furniture from the two men. I was quite happy with the house at that time but I didn't know what was to come!

The day we got the keys to the house, Henry was working late and so I moved in with what I could manage and made a meal for us. Henry wouldn't stay at the house though, as he hadn't sold his other house; so, I was four months pregnant and on my own in a huge house.

One weekend I went to collect Paul and told him that I had a surprise for him; when I turned into the drive he said "Mum, how could you?" I had no idea what he meant until he told me that his History teacher lived next door!

Henry had told me he had some furniture and boxes in storage, what he hadn't told me was how much. When his mum died he had put all of her furniture that he couldn't fit into his house, into storage. I was still excited at this stage, that excitement soon changed to despair when all of his storage goods were delivered; that day was a nightmare. Along with the four glass cabinets, huge sideboards, radiogram, tables and chairs were 100 boxes! I was frozen as I sat on the pew in the main hall, counting the boxes in and then cried. I was hurt and upset that he hadn't been honest with me.

His controlling nature was becoming very apparent; there was a very tall hedge separating the house from the pavement on the main road, much too high for us to manage ourselves and we decided that it would be best to have a few feet removed from the top. I arranged for that to happen and instead of being grateful that I had sorted that job out I was in big trouble with Henry. He said that he hadn't given me permission to sort it out! Warning signs are wonderful in hindsight! I put it down to the stress of having two houses as he was having trouble selling his other house - which in fact took three years.

My pregnancy was not going well. I kept having contractions from month five and had to be hospitalised on many occasions and dosed with Pethidine. It happened at work one day and I was taken to hospital, though on that occasion it was renal colic that had set off the contractions. I stayed in overnight, was released the next afternoon and back in hospital in the evening!

Even though Henry could see I was in some distress with the pregnancy it was still my job to tend to the vegetables on our little allotment, cope with the housework and maintain both cars. I was relieved when it was time to take my maternity leave but then worried as Henry insisted on me having the baby at home, he wanted four children and they all had to have natural births.

Henry and I wanted to arrange our wedding – it was only to be at the local registry office. The arrangement of the wedding proved to be difficult; Henry said that we had to be married at the right time 'astrologically' and to get a correct horoscope he needed my exact time of birth. I had no idea what that was, so against my wishes he phoned Joan; she had no idea either but Henry kept phoning her. I begged him to leave things alone but he is not a man to take 'no' for an answer. I found this out later on to my great cost. On one of these calls to Joan, we found out that my brother John was visiting from South Africa. He had flown over because Ron was very ill. I spoke with John who told me that Joan was dying of cancer, she was in a hospice and I should go and see her - I couldn't. I was still frightened and I was seven months into my pregnancy. I did visit Ron though, he was in Hope Hospital and he apologised to me for not doing anything about Joan's treatment of me – he was frightened of her as well.

Joan died on 4th February 1993 and Henry took me to her funeral. Henry and I were married soon after. The only member of my family to attend was my son Paul, he was 16 at the time. The day before our wedding I cleaned through the house and made all the food because the 'reception' was to be held at the house. I finally got into bed at 2.30am. The wedding was at 9.30am at the Register Office and there wasn't even any music as the system had just been stolen! After the 'ceremony' people came to our house for the reception. When the last person had gone, Henry went to bed and left me to clear up.

As I got closer to my time I prepared my bedroom and also the little bedroom – that meant that I had to move an awful lot of boxes – on my own.

Ben could not be born at home. The contractions started and Henry called the midwife out. Luckily I did have 'gas and air' in the house which I used to help ease the pain. When the midwife arrived she said that I needed to go to hospital and she had to insist upon that – Henry was not happy about it but my blood pressure had gone very high, as it had done at the end of my pregnancy with Paul. The ambulance arrived just as my 'gas and air' tank ran out. The journey to hospital was not comfortable for me. Henry followed behind in his car and said that a badger had run out in front of him so the baby had to be called 'Brock'! As the ambulance reached the hospital, the driver said to me "Where's maternity love?"

The baby was delivered normally but I was very bruised and had to have a catheter inserted into my bladder. I would not agree to the baby being called Brock and I chose the name Ben; Henry finally agreed to that after six weeks and on the last day for legally registering the baby's birth.

When Ben was only two weeks old Henry arranged for a French exchange student on work experience, to come and live with us, that meant that I had to move out of my bedroom. I now had someone else to look after and was feeling very isolated.

Communication with my family had again all but ceased and Ron moved into a nursing home in Leeds and later on to St Albans when Fiona and her family had moved there. I used to write to Ron but can only remember Rowena visiting me.

The French girl stayed with us for six months and, at first, I was relieved when she left. However, because there was no one else in the house Henry could behave as he really wanted to towards me. He became more intolerant, more demanding and nothing I did was right.

While the French girl was with us I slept in the same room as Ben and moved back into my own room as soon as she left.

Henry had been Vice Principal at a College but was made redundant. He embarked on a counselling course which meant even more work for me – typing up his assignments, etc., which were always on the last minute.

His behaviour became more bizarre, more controlling and more frightening. In the end it was easier to do as I was told. I returned to BNFL in October 1993 after having Ben but was pregnant again in December – not by choice. The event was a brutal violation of my body and totally degrading. Henry liked to tie my hands, over my head, to the bed, with blue twine – he used to keep it in his dressing gown pocket for those 'occasions'. My bedroom door did have a bolt at the top but he could get into my room from the 'library' via the shower room – that didn't have a lock or bolt and meant that I was vulnerable to his attacks. He made me 'dress up' for him – slave girl, school girl, etc., to do his bidding. I felt totally humiliated and degraded so that any love I had, or thought I had, for him was turned to fear and loathing. The 'rules' would change constantly so that I would always do something wrong.

This pregnancy was even worse than the previous one. I suffered regular contractions, lost weight and my symphysis pubis separated, I was given a 'belt' to tie round my hips to try and help matters but I could only walk with little steps. I was frequently in hospital because of the contractions and because my body kept going into ketosis; I was also very anaemic and had to have a blood transfusion at the 32 week stage. Henry insisted that I was 'making a meal of it'. I was off work more than I was in and I felt very isolated and unable to cope, with the demands of a young baby and Henry's increasingly strange behaviour.

After one set of tests I had a phone call from the hospital asking me to go right over. Henry was at college so I just bundled Ben into my car, a red Fiesta, and went straight over. The test had given a probability of 1 in 11 of my baby having Down's Syndrome and the staff wanted me to have an amniocentesis. If ever my calculations at work had given me that result, the project would be stopped! I agreed to have the investigation and then spoke to my GP and anyone I could about bringing up a child with that condition. The amniocentesis was carried out and I had three weeks to wait for the result – I was back in the hospital again when I got them – my baby was fine and was a girl, but I already knew that myself.

I had to get up at 5.30am to feed Ben before setting off to work. It had not been possible to find a suitable child-minder near home, so my only option was to engage a child-minder near work. I would then stay while Ben had his breakfast (3 Weetabix!) and then go to work, leaving as soon as possible after 4pm because my breasts were so full of milk and very uncomfortable.

As I was on sick-leave such a lot, BNFL decided to give me extended sick-leave. So I didn't have the awful journey to work and back but I was stuck at home with no help. One Tuesday I begged Henry not to go into college as I felt so unwell, I couldn't make Ben his breakfast and he just had biscuits. I had to phone my midwife in the afternoon, she called the doctor out and a neighbour came to look after Ben until Henry got back. He was not happy at having to leave college early and take me to hospital, he just would not accept that I was very ill. I think I was hoping that they would keep me in hospital for ever as I couldn't cope at all at home. Henry was totally wrapped up in his counselling course and there was still the problem of where this new baby was to sleep.

There was not enough room for a cot and a bed in the little bedroom so I had to move the boxes out of the other big bedroom onto the landing and move the cot in.

Next the boxes had to go in the smaller room. Ben was meant to sleep in a single bed and as he would only be 17 months old when the new baby came along I put cushions on the floor by the side of his bed.

Henry was always on the last minute with his assignments and expected me to type them up for him and would not let me go to bed until I had finished, even though I was heavily pregnant. One occasion I didn't get to bed until 2am and had to be at the hospital at 9.30am. The 'due' date for this baby was some time in September but she was born 8 days late.

I was so depressed and begged the consultant to 'get this baby out or I shall walk under a bus'. He was a very caring man and gave me a date to have the baby induced. I was pleased with that but Henry went totally mad and said that the baby had to be born at the right time 'astrologically'. He said that he would get an injunction to stop the induction! I was becoming more and more terrified of him and just had no idea what to do.

Fortunately my contractions started before the date for the induction and Henry drove me to hospital. My consultant would not agree to Henry's demand of another attempt at a home birth. The day after the baby was born, I decided to call her Gerry. The consultant said that Henry did not realise how much I had been suffering. I was back home after a few days in hospital and was totally exhausted – a friend did come over and stay for about a week. As he had done with Ben, Henry would not agree to Gerry's name unless she had certain other middle names and we had to visit Italy. I agreed to that but he still waited until the last possible day to register her birth.

When Gerry was four months old I suffered an early miscarriage; I was so pleased about that as I knew there was no way I could endure another pregnancy like the last two had been and I also knew that I did not have the strength to look after three babies, Henry and the house. Henry realised that I could not go through another pregnancy so he decided that I should have a coil fitted. I made the appointment at the surgery but the doctor was unable to fit the coil as I was too small and needed a smaller size of coil. Henry accepted that. When I went back for the next appointment and the doctor still could not fit the coil, Henry was not happy with me and insisted that I 'must have done something to stop it being fitted'. He would not take responsibility for birth control himself so I was accused of sabotaging his sex life. That was not to be allowed, so he took me over to the family planning clinic at the hospital and sat with me in the room whilst I had the coil fitted. He seemed to delight in the fact that I was in total agony.

Things started to get even worse with Henry, he wouldn't help me at all – he said that he had to study. I was due back at BNFL in April 1995 and could not find a child-minder to take on two babies. Henry was only at college on a Tuesday. He did have some work placements until he qualified and then worked at a local surgery, which is only a five minute drive or a 30 minute walk from home.

I was getting desperate for child care when I saw an advert in the local paper; a young girl, Mlada, (from the Czech Republic) was looking for au pair work. She moved in with us a few weeks before I was due back at work so that I could show her the routines: check ups with the health visitor, mums and tots groups, etc.

I had turned the old surgery room into a study and had my little word processor in there. I was still having to do all Henry's typing. One day I was in that study typing when I heard a great thud! I found Ben lying at the bottom of the stairs; he had been playing on the stairs with a ball. He had broken his leg.

I immediately sacked Mlada and saw my GP who gave me a sick note. She said that I was depressed anyway. BNFL's welfare officer came out to visit me and arranged for me to take voluntary redundancy. I received £23,000. Henry took £20,000 from me and let me keep the £3,000. Out of that I bought a washing machine and dryer; I was fed up with having to wash nappies in the butler's sink in the laundry room and washing the bedding was another nightmare.

Henry wanted us to go to Italy for a fortnight, so we booked a trip to Lido de Jesolo, a beach resort near Venice – but I had to pay for it out of the £3,000; as I had bought the washing machine, the dryer and a new mattress for my bed, paying for this holiday took the last of my money. Henry went to stay a couple of nights in Venice whilst we were in Lido de Jesolo, leaving me to cope with the two babies.

Henry decided that he needed more bookcases for the library and the landing so I was sent to get four of the tall bookcases from the local Argos store. My little red Fiesta and I had to make two trips. The staff in the store helped me get the bookcases into the boot, not an easy task. When all the bookcases were at the house, I then had to assemble them myself, which was not an easy task by myself, especially when they were taller than me!

We had put shelves up around two walls in the library and I 'found' that the only place that I could fit two bookcases was in front of the door into the shower room. I was so pleased with myself as that meant when

I bolted my bedroom door Henry could not get in through the shower room; that saved me from those sort of attacks but he took his revenge out on me in lots of other ways.

I wanted to decorate the study and that took me two weeks, even though it was small. Both babies got chicken-pox and there was all the other housework to be done. I did have a cleaner for a while until Henry used her to clean up his old house just before he managed to sell it. Then she stopped coming and I was back to square one.

The downstairs toilet was very damp and I had painted the walls so many times but the damp always came back. Henry's solution to this little problem was to block off the toilet! The damp was also in the laundry room. The cellar flooded when it rained and there was dry rot throughout the house which Henry just ignored. All the window frames were rotten and bits of timber kept falling from the roof.

At first I used to do my best in that house; cleaning the walls in the lounge and dining room with sugar soap, emptying boxes and trying to de-clutter the place. Henry would not help in any way and would not allow anything to be thrown out – even empty cardboard boxes, spices over 20 years old and a box of Tate & Lyle sugar cubes – priced at two shillings and sixpence! He criticised everything I did so in the end I gave up. He had, at that time driven me to take 16 overdoses by constantly telling me that I was useless, filthy, a disgrace, etc. One time I woke up in intensive care after three days in a coma and all he wanted to know was whether I had had a 'near death experience'.

My health visitor at that time suggested that I attend a course for women suffering 'post-natal depression'; I went along but I was the only person there! However, I did attend the self-esteem course. Gerry had to go in the crèche and screamed the whole time, but at least I was away from the house and Henry for a while. I must admit that I did not really benefit from the course as I was not a church goer at that time and it seemed to me that the message was 'to have self-esteem, one must have a faith'.

Despite Henry's claims later in court that I would not agree to go away on holiday we had plenty of vacations. Hay-on-Wye was one of his favourite places to go because of all the book shops – not very interesting for two babies though! We had a holiday in Turkey where he left me alone with Ben and Gerry while he went on a two night trip to Istanbul. While he was away I had a severe asthma attack and had to be treated in hospital; the hotel staff looked after the two babies until I was discharged.

My life was just a blur – looking after two babies, the huge house and Henry to contend with. I became more and more withdrawn and was still breastfeeding Gerry when she was 15 months old; Henry said that I did that to annoy him. I am not sure quite how it happened but I was taken into the psychiatric ward at the hospital. That is not a good place to be, if you are not ill when you go in, you certainly are when you get out. Whilst on the ward I kept a daily record of my feelings and events. When I read it over now I think to myself why didn't I leave Henry then? But where would I have gone? I had no money. Henry kept tight rein on the finances and I used to resort to taking £20 now and then from his wallet, (I knew where he hid it), to pay for the groceries.

The daily record I kept is Appendix 6.

Back Home after Discharge from Hospital

After I was discharged from the hospital I still had to attend during the week as a 'day patient'. This wasn't entirely satisfactory as I then had very little time for the housework so the arrangement was short lived.

I decided to work as a volunteer in the local Scope charity shop one day a week – Tuesday. That meant putting Ben and Gerry into the nursery school nearby; so it cost me a fortune to have the babies looked after whilst I worked for nothing all day! I worked there for three years. It was important to me, I was trying to get some self-confidence back and some independence.

When the children were able to walk I obviously wanted them to be able to play in the garden; that was forbidden by Henry on 'safety grounds'. Part of the garden by the garage backed onto the railway embankment and was not fenced off; that could have been easily rectified but he refused to do so. If the children wanted to play out, then I had to be with them all of the time.

When the children were at school (Ben) and pre-school (Gerry) Henry decided that I needed to go on a computer course, so I did the CLAIT course, and also Desktop Publishing. I would also try to get to the embroidery classes at the hospital on a Wednesday morning after which we ladies would then go for a pub lunch – such freedom!

I tried to have as normal a life as I could under difficult circumstances – i.e., not having a normal life!

I started to help at the children's school one morning a week – just general tasks like cleaning and sorting books, laminating – anything that needed to be done that the staff didn't have time for. This worked well until I turned up one morning to be told that 'Your husband phoned to change your day'. Just more controlling behaviour. I 'coped' with this by surrounding myself with 'bubble-wrap'; it's purpose was to cushion me from Henry's behaviour but it also cut me off from the world and it must have been very obvious to my friends at school that I needed help.

I was back under psychiatric care – I wasn't sleeping properly – a set of five tunes and songs kept going round and round in my head – it was like a ritual each night. I also started to 'hear' voices – it was as if the radio was on but not tuned in properly so that I couldn't make out what was being said. Henry said it was my mother trying to contact me to make up for her past behaviour towards me and to help me now. That made me feel even worse.

I tried attending a salon once a month for aromatherapy massage – I thought that it might relax me; it did – much to Henry's annoyance as he said that I was using it as a substitute for sex – I told him (in a rare moment of bravery) that it wasn't a substitute – it was better! Those little victories kept my sense of humour and kept me going.

Paul phoned one day to ask if his dad could buy the cooker which was in the garage, I said that he could have it in exchange for my piano; that was agreed and I had my piano back. I put it into the room that had been the surgery and began to teach Ben to play the piano – which he greatly enjoyed. Unfortunately, Henry did not enjoy this activity and decided that there was too much damp in that room and so he blocked it off and forbade me to play the piano, even going as far as hiding my music.

Eventually, in January 2001 I was taken back into hospital. I was told that I would be in for two weeks to adjust my medication. Those two weeks stretched into six months and involved even more medication and more ECT.

Henry never brought Paul over to see me whilst I was there but he would bring Ben and Gerry once a week. I did not keep a record of my time there – to me there didn't seem to be much point in doing anything. I felt that my life was over and indeed I wished it was. What the psychiatrists did not understand was that I wanted to be looked after, to be cared for, to be valued – all those things that husband and wife should receive from each other. I had expected to be loved, cherished and most of all respected but all I got from Henry was degradation and humiliation – according to him my degrees were worthless as they were 'only physics'. It was different when light bulbs needed to be changed and extension leads had to be sorted for the lawn mower – then he would say "You're the physicist – you do it".

During that time on the ward I was expected to attend classes – art, pottery etc. 'Art' meant colouring in – I became very adept at keeping in the lines but would occasionally have a mini revolution and colour outside the lines – what would the psychiatrists make of that? Pottery was a dismal failure – I threw my amorphous piece of clay across the room and never went back.

I became friendly with quite a few people whilst I was there, and we would enjoy winding the nursing staff up by discussing the best ways in which to commit suicide!

The police would often bring in people who had been found drunk in town. I do not understand why such people would be placed on a psychiatric ward. The women brought in such a state were trying to obliterate memories of their violent partners and were not criminals. Save the psychiatric wards for people who really need them, not sufferers of domestic abuse. We want to be protected, not put in more fear from other dangerous patients.

In a perverse sort of way I enjoyed being in hospital. At first I shared a room, the advantage of that was that I had en-suite facilities. When I was moved to a single room I was most put out. The staff could not understand this – the staff could not understand much – especially about me!

As the weather improved I was able to walk into town, usually with another patient. We would go into a café and have coffee and he always had a piece of cake. It was a very civilised time, then Henry would visit and spoil it all.

Part of the arrangement of being on psychiatric wards is that the patient should have some time at home to 're-adjust' – translated into my language that means going back to a living hell. A person from occupational therapy (OT) would be assigned to work with me, little outings into town, talks, and then visits back home. On most of my visits back to the house Henry would not be there and I was faced with housework. I don't mean housework, I mean washing the dishes. The kitchen was full of dirty dishes, etc., and so was the laundry room. There was no hot water and the kitchen sink was blocked – again. We had to keep boiling the kettle for hot water and it took my OT lady and myself two hours to clear up. Then it was time for me to be taken back to the ward and I hadn't seen Henry or the children.

I knew that I didn't want to go back to that house but what else could I do? I was given a date for discharge from the hospital and phoned some friends. They agreed to go to the house and make sure that it was OK for me to return to.

Whilst I was in the hospital I gave Henry my child benefit and incapacity books and asked him to pay my Barclaycard bill once a month, I generally paid £50 per month.

On my return home I asked for my benefit books back; he returned my incapacity book but refused to give me the child benefit book. He said that it was his money. I also discovered that he hadn't paid anything off my credit card – I therefore lost my account. He would not give me a reason for not paying that bill and I was then faced with an amount of £1700 to settle with Barclaycard. I tried to insist on having the child benefit book but he said that he had 'lost it'. As he also refused to complete the forms relating to my incapacity benefit, that was stopped as well.

I also discovered that during my six months in hospital he had scrapped my red Ford Fiesta car.

All this meant that I was completely dependent on Henry for money and had to ask him if I ever wanted to buy anything and I had to justify the intended purchase. He would give me £40 to do the week's grocery shopping and keep his car filled up with petrol!

Having spent six months in hospital I found it very difficult being at home and having to cope with Henry's stupid and bizarre behaviour. He would not allow anyone into the house to visit me, except the occupational therapists who were only allowed into a couple of rooms downstairs. He would dismantle the telephone when he went out and if he hadn't I was forbidden to answer it. One of the OT ladies was visiting me one day when the phone rang – she told me to answer it, I said I can't – she misunderstood and thought it was because she was there; when I explained she was dumbstruck. I didn't dare answer the phone in case it was Henry phoning to test me – if I had answered I would have been in serious trouble.

Trips out in the car, with Henry driving, would also be a nightmare; if he saw a jogger he would beep the car horn - 'to make the jogger break step!' At a certain crossroads he would insist on signalling right when he was actually going straight on – that would totally confuse other drivers and frighten me – it was a huge joke to him. He seemed to gain some sort of perverse satisfaction from his mind games on me and other people.

Gerry needed a new coat and I knew that there was a sale on at Woolworth's so I asked Henry for some money to buy one for her – he was still in bed – and told me to send her up to him to 'state her case for requiring a new coat'! She was eight years old! However, he gave me some money and Gerry chose a gold, shiny duffel coat. When she showed her dad he said 'You look like a street walker – go back and change it'. I refused to do that and she kept the coat; my little victories were mounting up.

Everybody is aware that I like the colour pink, so Henry would do his best to ruin my pink clothes – he bleached my nice pink striped towels and said it was an 'accident'. He would also set me 'tests' with the washing up; he would ask if I had done that job and I would say that I had. Silly me – I would then be dragged into the kitchen to be shown a great load of glasses that he had put in a black bin-liner – in the oven! Of course that trick only worked that one time as I would check everywhere for dirty pots.

My way of coping with all of this was to go back to bed when I had taken the children to school. I would set my radio alarm for 2.30pm and take four sleeping tablets. I would collect the children from school and then make the evening meal – that of course had to be made from scratch, ready meals were not allowed - I still don't use them now but that is by choice. Even then the meals I made were never good enough for Henry.

The house was impossible to keep clean because of all Henry's rubbish – he would not throw anything away and when he asked me why I hadn't vacuumed the carpet in his library, my only answer was that I could not see the carpet! It would take me two hours to hoover in the living room for a couple of reasons – the room was very large and the hoover was not up to the job; I started to clean the walls in the living and dining rooms with sugar soap – that job took me several weeks to complete.

I was referred by my psychiatrist to a Professor. He changed some of my medication (that makes them feel better, not the patient) and told me to stay out of bed during the day. I started to do that – first by watching some TV, then reading magazines, then novels, then doing crosswords and puzzles. Henry's response to this was "Shouldn't you be in bed?"

One Sunday afternoon the children and I had been gardening, when we had finished I took them inside to give them a bath. Henry was in bed in his room and when I opened the door to the bathroom I found the ceiling in the bath and all over the floor; I asked Ben to tell his dad what had happened and Henry's reply was "I know, I've left it for you to clean up"!

I can remember one tea time Henry suddenly put down his knife and fork, turned to Ben and said "If anything happens to me you must report your mother to the police!" I have no idea why he said that – it just came out of the blue and I could not respond; maybe it was just another way of turning Ben against me or was Henry getting scared himself – knowing that he was pushing me too far?

Shopping trips with Henry were not enjoyable experiences either. One day I hadn't packed the goods into the boot of the car quick enough and he slammed the boot down on me – my GP, health visitor and DV Support worker all saw the bruises and documented the incident.

The house in Buxton caused me more problems as my name had not been removed from the documents as I had thought and when Arthur died suddenly I was left with a huge debt. The house had to be sold and I was trying to sell the furniture – I had brought some very good items, a mahogany dining table and chairs and a matching dresser were among the best items. Henry took those and put them in the garage and forbade me to sell them. He had absolutely no right to do that but I felt powerless.

Leaving Henry

Life was wonderful when Henry was out of the house and when he went away to London and Edinburgh for the festival which he attended each year. He would claim that I was incapable of looking after the children but amazingly it didn't worry him when he went off on his weekends and weeks away! He said that he knew when I was ill or OK – perhaps his astrological charts or tarot cards told him, how convenient!

The children and I dreaded the time when Henry returned from work. He would hammer on a window in the living room – I suppose that at least gave us warning and a chance to prepare ourselves. The children would hide their biscuits (if they were eating one) under the cushions of the settee and turn off the TV. I would open the door for Henry and he would come into the living room, scoop everything off the coffee table by his armchair and then complain about the mess on the floor. My pathetic attempts at trying to say "But you have just done that" would be met with a slap or a good throttling, he very much liked to have his hands around my neck – I wasn't so enthusiastic.

In October I asked Henry if he would come to counselling with me to try and sort out our marriage but he told me that any 'problems' were all in my head. His behaviour was such that I took another overdose and it was while in hospital that I decided my only course of action was to leave him. When I talked to the children about leaving, Gerry asked if she could bring her cuddly toys and Ben wanted to know if he could walk home from school with his mates.

After a particularly nasty incident with Henry I ran across the road to the doctor's surgery and asked for help. My GP was wonderful, he brought in the Health Visitor and she in turn brought in a lady from the Domestic Violence Outreach service.

I owe those people my life and I am forever grateful. I still think of, and miss, the woman from Domestic Violence Outreach who worked with me for 3 years.

The first thing I was advised to do was to get a mobile phone and not let Henry know about it. I also went to CAB (Citizens Advice Bureau) and they managed to get me two years back pay of Child Benefit and about ten months Incapacity Benefit. This money was paid into my Post Office account; I withdrew it all, paid off the credit card bill and put the rest into the Royal Bank of Scotland – a friend said to me, "If he finds that money in your drawer, you are dead!" She took me straight round to the bank on the corner. I saw my health visitor and domestic violence support worker on a weekly basis and with their help decided to look for somewhere else to live.

On Friday 5th December 2003 I took possession of a 3 bed house, it was just across the road from the children's' school.

On Thursday 18th December I had to be at my new house for 9am as the man from Income Support was coming to interview me and the dining table and chairs were to be delivered. Henry took Gerry to school but Ben was not well and had to stay home. I phoned a friend and she came to look after Ben whilst I got the bus to my new house.

My friend arrived at the same time as the man from Income Support, she also brought an armchair for me. Ben explored the house while I was being interviewed – it only took about 20 minutes. The dining table then arrived and Ben asked if he could have football nets in the garden – I obviously agreed to that. We then went back to the family home to collect some of my belongings and Ben became very upset, phoned Henry and locked himself in the bathroom. My friend took the keys to my new house and took my things there. Ben eventually came out of the bathroom and was in the lounge with me when two police officers walked in. The policeman took Ben upstairs while the policewoman talked to me. The next thing was Henry banging on the window and demanding to talk to the policewoman privately. One of my friends arrived – she said that she had followed the police into the drive and had spoken to them about what had been going on.

Everybody then came outside and Henry said that he wanted me to leave right away. The policewoman said that he was a bully and that I had every right to stay. I didn't see that I actually had much choice so I grabbed a few belongings from my room and left with my friend. Ben stayed with Henry; the police had advised me to collect Gerry from school and take her to my new house. I telephoned the school, explained the situation and took Gerry to our new home. Gerry put the legs on the dining table and another friend called round with lots of household things for me and I then managed to make some tea.

About 5.30pm a different police officer arrived; he told Gerry to put her coat on and go outside to Henry – I was furious with him – especially when he began to tell me that I wasn't capable of looking after my children because of my 'mental health'. Fortunately one of my friends returned and after she had talked with him, the police officer he left.

Henry collected Gerry on the morning of 25th December 2003 so that she could spend Christmas with her dad and Ben. He gave me a letter saying that he would return her to me on Friday 2nd January 2004.

THAT NEVER HAPPENED.

I was totally distraught; it is very easy for people reading this to think I was stupid in letting Gerry go but Henry gave me a letter and his word – and I was obviously extremely naïve in trusting him; I would never make that mistake again. Henry did let me speak briefly with Gerry; she said that she 'wasn't allowed' to see me any more.

The school term resumed on Monday 5th January but the children did not attend that week. On the evening of 5th January I was presented with court papers which stated that 'Interim custody had been granted to Henry'. I was forbidden to remove them from school or their father's house and a date had been set for a 15 minute hearing in court on 12th January at 11.10am. It was at that hearing that I was granted telephone contact with Ben and Gerry – I was to phone them each evening at 6.30pm.

Apparently, Henry had paid to go before a judge claiming that I was a mentally ill alcoholic; on Henry's word ONLY was the ex-parte order for interim custody made. I had also been seeing a solicitor and cannot understand why I was never told that interim custody orders could be made – I would have found the money from somewhere/someone. Still, I wasn't told and have been fighting that court order ever since – always one step behind and always being on the defensive.

I have kept detailed journals from the half-term before leaving Henry but the main point is that the court case lasted for three years until I was eventually given the divorce and a pittance of a settlement out of which I had to pay back the so called 'legal aid' of £23K.

The reports submitted by my psychiatrist and other professionals were never taken into account. I do not believe that they were even read by the judge – he/she may have been worried that his/her original ruling was wrong.

One unusual encounter I had was early in February 2004, before one of the court cases; I went to see a clinical hypnotherapist; I needed to find some extra strength to face the upcoming events. During the session we talked for a long time about my situation, Henry's behaviour over the years and, of course, the court hearing on 18th February. When I told the therapist that Henry was a counsellor he laughed and said that all counsellors are wasting their time as they only deal with the conscious mind. He also said that Henry's behaviour suggested that he suffered from Asperger's Syndrome and that the problem was therefore with him and not me! The actual hypnotherapy session was amazing; I was fully aware of what was going on but felt absolutely stuck to the chair. The therapist told me that during the court hearing I would be calm and controlled and that I wouldn't let anything Henry said get to me – he told me that I could 'let it all out' once I got home.

At first I was granted telephone contact with Ben and Gerry – I was to phone them at 6.30pm each evening; this lasted until the next court case held on 18th February 2004, in which the barrister stated that was ridiculous. The children were then able to visit me after school, a couple of times a week and could stay with me on alternate weekends.

Henry was not happy with any of these arrangements and did his best to ruin them – the children were never 'available' to speak with me on the telephone and he would never bring a change of clothes for them at the weekends.

How did I keep myself sane whilst all this was going on? By seeing my DV (Domestic Violence) Support Worker once a week. She was wonderful. Sometimes we would just talk about 'Star Trek' (Data was one of her favourite characters), I would see myself as Captain Janeway! I also saw my GP and health visitor regularly; my GP would just talk with me or just listen to me. He knew how I felt about taking medication and I was trying to come off all the horrible drugs – Lithium, Prozac, Chlorpromazine, Mirtazipine, sleeping tablets, etc., It took me about two years to come off them all and I am very proud of myself for doing so.

The stress of all the court cases and dealings with Henry would have been a great excuse to remain on the medication. I found strength in other ways, ways that I would never have dreamed of before.

Some time after the court case, I received a telephone call from social services telling me that, I should telephone the police if I suspected that the children are on their own in the house. I was also advised that I should be able to see my children and that Henry has no right to stop me. That was fine for social services to say but they never did anything to help me regarding the children; the 6.30pm telephone calls to the children were usually very upsetting as either they refused to speak with me, Henry wouldn't let them speak with me or he wouldn't answer the telephone.

One of my friends who had helped me escape, worked at the local playgroup and she said that I should work there a couple of sessions a week as a volunteer. The arrangement worked very well and I was asked to become member of staff – that was a boost to my ego! I also started to go to belly dance classes. Another source of strength was attending 'The Freedom Programme' at The Women's Centre until July 2004– it was a course for women who had suffered any form of domestic abuse, however, even at that group I could not tell anyone about the sexual abuse, I was still too ashamed. Henry's taunts of 'that's what wives are for' and 'no-one will ever believe you', still ring loud in my ears.

So, I was growing in self-esteem without the aid of psychiatric medication; I also started to lose weight which had gone up to nearly 14 stone from being under 9 stone after having the babies.

Henry was incredibly difficult about allowing me to collect my belongings and in the end I had to go to the house with a woman PC. When Henry opened the door he put his hand out as if stopping traffic and took the WPC inside, a few moments later I was allowed entry. He had obviously given her the 'mental health' spiel as she was most unpleasant with me: 'Hurry up, I don't have much time to waste here'. How could I hurry? The rooms were in such a mess with papers and books scattered randomly about, that it would have taken hours to find anything; of course I was not allowed to move his 'sorted' papers which were placed over my belongings. I gathered together the few bits that I could – I wanted my music and my degree notes but could not find them anywhere. I also wanted my clogs, two pairs from when I danced with 'Clever Clogs'; I never found those either.

On one of the children's visits, Gerry, only ten years old, told me a very disturbing tale:- she said that for a couple of years she had been seeing dead people in the house. She said that they chased her and she sees them dead on the floor – in the living room and the big hall. The murderer came at her in the hall and stabbed her in the back, she says that she is still alive because he was a ghost. She also says that she sees 'Izzy' who is 14 years old and has long, ginger, wavy hair and wears clothes like Dorothy in The Wizard of Oz. Izzy watches Gerry and the family and protects them sometimes; but sometimes she is mean to Gerry and traps her. I found this quite disturbing, to say the least, especially when I found out that Henry had told Gerry that she is Izzy and that she is seeing into the future. Gerry persisted with the story of dead people and told me that she wanted to go to a spiritualist church to get in touch with Henry's mum.

The visits and telephone calls continued to be erratic and at times upsetting. Sometimes though things were wonderful. The children could play out in the garden (something which was never allowed at their father's) and have their friends visit for tea, games and sleepovers.

Henry had no interest in raising the children, he only wanted to stop me from seeing them; part of my punishment for daring to leave him. A great many of his outbursts were carried out in front of the children and because of this Ben thought that was the correct way to behave. The children were treated differently by Henry; he said that he was training Gerry to be a 'good little housewife'. Ben would himself be on the receiving end of Henry's violence by being kicked and punched by him; I would intervene, to my cost. He was still trying to undermine me and ridicule everything I did or wanted to do. One example was when I asked the children if they would like to make some bread, Henry told them, 'your mother isn't capable'.

Every Easter in the local park, there are trails put on for children and as the children were to spend the week with me I took them. Ben really enjoyed solving the clues and moving on to the next one, the whole walk took about an hour and a half. The reward at the end was of course an Easter egg each. Henry had refused to bring suitable shoes for them to walk in as he didn't agree with me taking them on a walk! My friends came to my rescue once again.

The children also spent a week in June with me, that coincided with my 50th birthday and so I held a party. Henry did his best to ruin it by constantly 'phoning and demanding to speak with the children. They were having far too good a time playing with their friends and refused to come to the phone; he was not pleased. Paul, my eldest son, came to the party with his dad, that was the last time I saw Chris.

July did bring complaints from school about Ben's behaviour towards the staff, especially the female staff. Shortly after that Ben was aggressive to me and then ran off making Gerry go with him.

The rest of the year was spent in court, seeing social services, a CAFCASS (Children and Family Court Advisory and Support Service) officer and a child psychologist; I was becoming worn down by the whole situation. I never knew how the children would behave with me and when, sometime before Christmas a card from the local churches came through the door, I telephoned the vicar of the local church. He invited me over to the vicarage to have a good talk with him and suggested that I start attending the services and meet some more people. The only people I knew locally were other mums and so during school holidays I was quite lonely.

My first visit to a church service (of my own volition) was on Sunday 19th December. I was fine when I arrived but during the service I just sobbed and sobbed. I had sat in the first place I saw which was next to a couple called Tim and Yvonne, we were to become good friends. I had coffee with them after the service and went home thinking that I would not be able to face going back.

I was back in court on 22nd December and contact over Christmas was arranged; no overnight stays. At the end of December I was advised by my solicitor to give up with residence proceedings, I very reluctantly agreed to that but the children were absolutely adamant that they wanted to stay with Henry. The solicitor said she would then be able to concentrate on getting help for the children; that didn't happen either and I felt tricked.

A late, and very welcome but unexpected present arrived at the end of the year – a cheque for £2000 from The Murdoch Charitable Trust; that was a much needed boost to my finances and enabled me to buy a small car. I had forgotten about replying to an advert in the CAB office a year earlier.

The start of another year

I applied for (and was appointed) a job as support worker for a mental health team – I could understand a lot of what was needed from that job – mostly someone to listen to you and a bit of help with practicalities – benefits being top of the list. Why has the government made claiming one's entitlements so difficult?

I accepted the job as part of the government's 'New Deal for over 50's; the condition was that weekly hours worked had to be kept to under 15. That way I would not lose all my benefits. Despite that rule, I received a very nasty letter from the Incapacity Benefit agency telling me that they had been 'informed of my fraudulent claim' and I was to be interviewed 'under caution'! I was absolutely furious with them, and told them so; I never received an apology and I suspect it was another of Henry's little games.

I started the support work in January 2005 and also bought myself a little car, (£795), it was very necessary as I was to be visiting clients all over the area and also had to take them out. My car was a blue Cinquecento called Pearl (she was a little gem!). Henry also told the children that they were not to get into my car because, 'your mother is such a terrible driver'. I ignored him, another of his attempted put-downs.

The father of my eldest son died suddenly on 19th January and all I could think was 'why wasn't it Henry?'

As the contact visits with the children seemed to be going quite well and they knew that they would be with me for a week in August (Henry always attends the Edinburgh Festival), we looked through some holiday brochures and chose a week at Pontin's in Prestatyn. I then booked and paid for that. When August came

Henry would not allow the children to come with me.

This year (2005) I was in court on 6 occasions – always with a different barrister, that doesn't help; if you are in receipt of 'legal aid' (really a loan) it seems you just have to take pot luck with your legal advisers. If I had known that at the time I would have paid up front and engaged a good barrister myself.

As I was getting more work at the agency I decided to leave playgroup at the end of the spring term.

On one of Gerry's visits, she wanted to shower and wash her hair as she was going to a sleepover at one of her friends. Whilst drying her hair I found it to be full of nits and more worrying, bruises on her arms and legs. She said that she had 'bumped into something'! How many victims of abuse have used that explanation? I did try to tell Henry about the nits in her hair but he just told me to 'shut up'.

It was during the spring of 2005 that I started to have trouble with my elbows. My GP diagnosed 'tennis elbow' but I am still suffering with the pain even now. He even gave me an injection which made everything worse! By this time I was also off all the nasty psychiatric medication and my GP was very pleased – he said that I was a different woman from a year ago. My psychiatrist was not so happy when I told her though! She should have been pleased – are these people in the pay of the drug companies?

Gerry turned up at my house unexpectedly on 3rd March at 3.30pm. Henry hadn't collected her. I phoned both his land line and his mobile and left messages. He called back and said that he was 'on his way'. When he arrived I asked him where he had been – he smirked and said that he had been 'on the phone' and that Gerry is supposed to walk home alone if he doesn't turn up; he was very angry that she had come to me. It is a 45 minute walk along the busy road from my house to her dad's; I was informed afterwards that Gerry regularly does that walk. When she visits me she likes me to wash her hair and have a shower. She told me that her dad only allows her to shower once a week. She was a ten year old girl and personal hygiene was a big issue, especially as puberty was looming. Henry would not have had a clue as to how to help her through that.

In April I visited Ben's school and the most helpful member of staff there, was the Head of Science who suggested that I contact the school nurse, and the English teacher who also shared my concerns about Ben's poor social skills and challenging behaviour. I then met with the school nurse at the end of April, she was very understanding and said that she would contact someone at Family Liaison.

The contact visits with Gerry were becoming very pleasant despite Henry's attempts to sabotage them. Ben was still being very 'demanding'. The events of the evening of Saturday 14th May were to change everything though.

I collected Gerry from school at 3.15 on Friday 13th. She had arranged for two of her friends to sleep over. Then two other friends arrived to play and on his arrival, Ben wanted to know, 'what is going on?' He called a friend of his to come over. I made a roast chicken dinner for everyone followed by fresh fruit and yoghurt. The girls slept in the living room – on the sofa, the futon and an air-bed. At midnight they wanted tuna and pasta and at 2am they said that they were 'tidying up'! They did finally get some sleep.

In the morning I took Ben, Gerry and the girls into town and we had a pleasant day together. Gerry asked if she could stay over with me again. I phoned Henry who was very unpleasant and said that she had to go back. Gerry was upset at that so she phoned him but he still refused to allow her to stay with me. Gerry was equally determined that she was staying "Why should I go back and be bored when I can stay here and have fun?"

I didn't really know what to do for the best and so Gerry went over to her friend's house with her. Henry arrived at 6pm and was aggressive, threatening and saying that he would call the police. I told him that I had already spoken with the police and they did not want to get involved in a 'civil matter'. The police are also very good at lying!

Gerry chose to stay at her friend's house that night so I went back home and locked myself in – I didn't know what her dad would do. At around 7.30pm the police broke down my back door and searched the house; they said that my husband had informed them that I had 'kidnapped' Gerry. When they realised that she wasn't in the house, (I kept telling them that she was at a friends house – which Henry well knew) they threatened to arrest me for wasting their time! I went to my next door neighbours for help as the police were extremely unpleasant (two female and one male officers). One of the police officers even told me that the way Henry had taken the children from me 'could not have happened'.

I phoned the Domestic Violence Unit and left a message for the officers who had been working with me.
My landlord had to be informed about the damage to the back door and he was appalled. When I phoned at 6.30 to speak with the children, Henry said that Gerry would not be coming to me on Monday. I also spoke with my health visitor, she phoned the police and told them that I

needed support, not intimidation.

I contacted my solicitor and was advised to inform Gerry's school and Social Services about the incident. The Headmistress wanted a copy of the court order outlining the contact details so I took that over to her office. Henry had booked Gerry into the after school club (she should have been with me). Gerry was brought to the headmistress's office and was clearly very distressed and frightened. Henry had forbidden her to come home with me and I had no alternative but to let her go back to the club. God knows what he said and did to her. She was terrified and so was I.

My outreach worker phoned to give me support and also my health visitor who said that she would contact social services and urged me to lodge a complaint. I had already done that – on-line.

The two domestic violence unit officers came to see me on Tuesday and also took copies of the contact order, which they said they would send to all the local police stations. They said that Henry is 'evil'. They also helped me to change solicitors.

The lady from Family Liaison phoned me to say that Ben's school would not allow her to work with him – was it the school or was it Henry? She said that she would try to help via social services and also try to help Gerry.

An inspector phoned me on Friday to say that he was handling my complaint and that he had spoken with the Domestic Violence Unit. He later backed up his officers by saying that they 'acted to preserve life'! On top of all this my benefits were stopped and I had to apply for Working Tax Credits!

Everything was going against me. I suppose it was a good thing that I did have the support work to keep me occupied – even if some of my clients were 'challenging'.

I kept trying to phone the children (the 6.30pm phone calls had never been stopped) but Henry was obstructive and even said one time that, 'as he didn't like the letter from my solicitor about the 'incident' and that I had not shown 'any remorse' then the children would not be coming to me.

My new solicitor told me that as the contact order is still in place that I should collect Gerry from school on the appropriate days. I did so the following Monday (23rd May) – Henry had booked her into the after school club again. Gerry was more than happy to come home with me, we worked on my computer and printed off pictures of pyramids for her talk on Egypt. Henry collected her at 6pm and never said a word.

A letter arrived for me from my local MP, asking for my permission to contact the police about the incident. I managed to speak with Ben who told me that he didn't come to me as. 'dad told me not to'.

I had an appointment with the Headteacher at Ben's school who was very apologetic that Ben's Head of Year tutor had insisted on a letter from my solicitor regarding Parental Responsibility. She also agreed to send me copies of any reports and activities.

Henry would not allow the children to come to me for the weekend nor the following weekend. He left a message on my land line to say that they were in Norfolk for a week. I seized my chance and went straight over to the house and managed to get some more of my personal belongings. The house was in such a disgusting state that I decided to take photographs as evidence of how he was 'caring' for the children. Armed with this information I approached social services, NSPCC and environmental health. No one was interested – if animals were living in those conditions they would have stepped in straight away – but as it's only children it doesn't matter. Ian (my husband) later suggested that I should have contacted the RSPCA and told about the cruelty to mice and frogs that lived in the cellar!

Because of the 'police incident' I was back in court on 15th June 2005 and a new contact order was set. Tuesdays after school until 7pm and alternate Saturdays, 11am – 7pm. No overnight stays! Then, on 28th June, I was back in court for the finances. My arms were hurting so much and my weight was down to 11st 6lbs.

Then, more bad news, my Housing Benefit was stopped. Too add to this, Gerry was not coping well with the situation and was being 'difficult' at school. I also received a copy of the CAFCASS report which stated that, the children have said that they are afraid to go on holiday with me because of my 'alcohol abuse' and 'mental health problems'. I was appalled. I really could not believe that Henry could, and did, make the children say such things about me. A few weeks later I asked Ben why he had said such things and he replied that 'It was just a joke!' Henry was more than happy to leave me with the children whilst he went to London, Edinburgh, etc. He also said that they were too embarrassed to be with me because of my 'hideous appearance'. My solicitor and barrister were not impressed with the CAFCASS report and neither was the judge, but she would not enforce the holiday I had booked with the children for August. The Pontin's holiday was booked because Henry wanted me to have the children from 13th - 20th August 2005 which coincidentally was the week of the Edinburgh Festival. However, since the police 'incident' Henry has not allowed me to see Ben at all.

Ben was extremely unpleasant with me after this last court hearing and even Gerry left a message on my land line saying that 'If I turned up at school she would call the cops and have me arrested'! This was a complete turn around in Gerry's attitude and I found it very distressing. Her school teachers also told me that her attitude was 'going the same way as Ben's'. However, I still managed to persuade my psychiatrist to discharge me.

The children did come for a visit on Wednesday 27th July and were both very badly behaved but were extremely pleasant when we spoke the next day. The visit from them on 2nd August was another bad time – Ben broke the garage window because I stopped him from hurting Gerry.

My situation at work was improving; I had my probationary interview on 12th August and was given a new 25 hour/week contract (10 hours more than I was doing). I was told that everyone was very happy with the way in which I support my clients. That was a well needed boost to my self-esteem and I gave in my resignation at playgroup. The next day was the start of my 'Pontin's week; I had decided that I might as well go (I couldn't get my money back) and a friend was to join me from Wednesday with one of her children.
I did try to keep up the 6.30pm telephone calls to the children but never managed to speak with them. One night Henry left a message on my mobile to say that 'telephone contact does NOT take place during holidays as the children needed a break from them!' Nowhere in the court order was that written. The man is a total liar and has no regard for the courts, or anyone in fact. He

thinks that he can lay down the rules for contact. I just want to know how he managed (and seemingly, was allowed) to get away with it.

Ben and Gerry did speak with me when I had returned home and told me that they had been to a PGL holiday at Shrewsbury. That cannot have been arranged at the last moment so Henry never had intention of letting the children come away on holiday with me – he was just trying to mess things up for me – again.

During the week I started 'Belly Dance' classes, (Yvonne from church started to come with me as well). I also went to the hospital to have an 'appliance' fitted on my elbow – it was too large and so a smaller one was ordered. I also had an interview at 'Adoption Counselling' as I wanted to get a copy of my full birth certificate. The full certificate arrived on 2nd September.

The contact visits were going well, though one time Ben did say that Henry had forbidden me to eat red meat! I told Ben that I would eat whatever I chose. The visit on 6th September however, was a disaster; Ben was very rude to me and tried his best to break all the doors in the house. I was speaking with Paul when the children ran off and I kept driving round to find them. I did locate them but they just kept running off. I tried to phone Henry but he wasn't answering any phone so I had no choice but to actually go to his house. I rang the doorbell until he answered – his response when I told him about the children was 'What have you done to them now?' Paul later let me know that the children were back home – I won't say 'safe' because I don't believe anyone is safe with Henry. The next day Gerry apologised for running off; I told her never to do that again as I was very worried and upset.

It was during this week that I went to church one evening for a 'Sing & Sip' session, a glass of wine followed by hymn singing; that meant that I was now a member of the church singing group which practises every Thursday evening for an hour and sings at church on the first Sunday of every month. I also somehow became the 'prompt' for the church pantomime. The confirmation classes had also started so I was getting really busy with church activities.

I had to attend another CAFCASS interview on 20th September (they had wanted to interview myself and Henry together but I would not agree to that). Ben was now refusing to even to talk with me on the telephone and would not visit me. When Henry collected Gerry at 7pm he started 'kerb crawling' and staring at me in the way that meant 'trouble is coming'.

Soon Henry's financial declaration and statement arrived and was an incredible piece of work. He thinks that as I may inherit money/assets from my natural father (who died in the 1970's), that he doesn't need to pay me any form of settlement! He later added another demand:- that any sum he has paid me is to be repaid if I remarry, cohabit or die! My solicitor said that she had never seen such a request.

Ben was still refusing to see me or even speak with me and Gerry was very variable. I was also starting to have a few challenges at work with one of my clients. The lady was suffering from schizophrenia and her husband was quite abusive. After a particularly awful session I asked for someone else to take over her support, I didn't feel safe visiting her.

My friend, Liz, came with me on my weekend trip to Barrow. I was going to try to locate the church in which I had been baptised, as I now had my full birth certificate and knew where Joan had been living when I was born. I spent all Saturday in the library whilst Liz went to visit her uncle in Ulverston. All my investigations showed that I was not baptised in the Church of England and the Catholic Churches do not issue public records. Once back home, I phoned the nearest Catholic Church to where Joan had been living; I explained to the priest that I needed my baptism certificate for my confirmation in December. He phoned back within two hours to say that he had found me and would send all the details to my vicar. I had been baptised on 11th July 1954 at St Mary's on Duke Street, Barrow.

As well as having trouble with my arms, my neck was also hurting and an x-ray showed that I have stage 2, chronic degeneration of three cervical vertebrae.

My solicitor had arranged for me to see a barrister on 20th October, who said that Henry was talking nonsense when he said that I am only entitled to 5% of the value of the house. He also said that he would use the photographs of the state of the house and that I hadn't committed any crime by entering the house.

Towards the end of October I received a letter from Housing Benefit informing me that as the children no longer lived with me I did not need this 3 bedroomed house. I let my landlord know about this situation and he wrote me an 'eviction letter' to include with my claim for housing benefit. At a consultation with my GP, to hurry up my hospital appointment for my elbows I brought him up to date with court events. I told him that I wanted to shoot Henry– my GP said that wasn't a very good idea and that anyway there were plenty of people at the surgery who would gladly shoot him for me!

My role as a support worker was becoming quite stressful, since the arrival of a new manager. His planning had me in three places at the same time and I had to point out to him that was not possible.

Gerry was upset that Henry would not allow her to go to the school disco. He also refused to let me speak with her one evening as she had a tummy upset; he said it was because I had made her ill with my cooking. Her tummy upset was more than likely to have come from the food she had eaten at the bonfire, that Henry had taken her to, so I threw the accusation back at him and was shaking afterwards. When I next spoke with Gerry she asked 'Why did you poison me?' and stated that she would not be eating any more of 'my awful food'. After speaking with the other mums and school, I was assured that there was indeed a 'tummy bug' doing the rounds. Henry would just use anything against me and do his best to jeopardise my relationship with Gerry – just as he had done with Ben.

I was back in court on 8th November and expected to see the barrister I had met with previously; apparently he was busy on a different case and another woman barrister had come to represent me. She was not very nice at all and was not happy that I had a friend and also my DV support worker with me. I told her that I needed an urgent interim payment from Henry but she said that wasn't possible. I kept telling her that I only had £25 in my purse to last me until 15th November; I am sure that she did not believe me. I then told her that if I don't get any money, I would have to move back into the house with Henry and she said that I was entitled to do so. She then turned to my DV support worker and asked her if that would be safe for me. The answer was 'of course it wouldn't be safe – but Lynne is trying to show you how desperate she is'. The barrister suggested that I just move into a little flat. If I did that, then the children would never be able to stay overnight with me and also I had made a lovely little home for myself (and the children) and had a very good support network in friends and church.

This barrister wanted me to stop the court case and just accept the pathetic amount of contact that I had with Gerry, Ben was still being difficult. I absolutely refused to do that and told her that if she didn't put my case before the judge, I would show her the photographs of the state of the house. The barrister went before the judge and said that she believed that Henry was NOT encouraging contact; the judge said 'I know, but how do I prove it?' Surely, it is not up to the judge to prove such things. I had given my solicitors and barristers all the evidence that was required.

After that encounter with the judge I collapsed – a result of stress, no sleep and no food. My friend who was with me suggested that I collect Gerry from school and bring her round to her house for tea; Gerry enjoyed that.

As I was struggling to pay the rent, my health visitor suggested that I apply for council accommodation in the village where my children were and where I had lived for 11 years. She helped me with the application, but I was turned down on the grounds that 'I had no connection with that village'! I was outraged – how do people from overseas get housing when they cannot possibly have any connections to any place in the UK?

There was another 'incident' on Friday 11th November. I was on my four hour support visit with my client and we had just adjourned to a café for lunch. My soup had just arrived when my mobile rang, it was the Primary School letting me know that Gerry had been sick that morning and had no lunch with her. They had been unable to contact Henry and wanted me to collect Gerry. This was at 1.45pm; I made a quick call to work, asked the café to put my soup in a take away container and drove to school. I gave Gerry my soup whilst I phoned my solicitor. Gerry then ate a cheese and tomato bap, a banana and drank a hot chocolate – she was ravenous. The school nurse rang me whilst Gerry was eating and offered to set up a 'Child in Need' meeting. Henry would have to be invited. I was very pleased at this suggestion as I thought it would mean that all my concerns over Gerry's welfare would now be documented formally.

Henry collected Gerry at 3.30pm and never said a word.

At work I was given another client who was still on the psychiatric ward. She was to be another difficult case. My journal states that I was 'feeling terrible' at this time. My arms were giving me a great deal of pain and I was also feeling exhausted. I collapsed at the belly dance class the following Monday evening and ended up at the hospital. They found that my blood pressure was high and that I was 'stressed'! My friends from church were with me and got me home safely. I was getting really worried about being ill as Henry was demanding access to my medical records.

At the end of November 2005 I had a message from the school nurse to say that she had managed to set up a 'Child in Need meeting' on 5th December. Those attending were Social Services, CAFCASS, child protection and my health visitor. Henry had been informed and was not pleased. I was then feeling very frightened but also thought that someone must listen to me.

A side effect of all this was that my blood pressure was getting high (142/99) and I was signed off work on sick leave. Henry would not understand that the 'Child in Need meeting' was about welfare, not contact. I was also prescribed beta-blockers and told not to lose any more weight for the moment (I had dropped to 10st 4lbs).

I had a back massage at the local salon but it really hurt; the facial was very relaxing though and I nearly fell asleep. My doctor also doubled my beta-blockers.

Saturday, 3rd December was the day of the pantomime and Gerry really enjoyed herself with me that day, she sat with me whilst I prompted and then got up on stage at the end to dance. The drama group then held their Christmas party on Sunday 4th December and my vicar had to walk me home! The 'Child in Need meeting' was the next day and I was terrified.

The meeting was at 10am; Henry was 10 minutes late, he was then awkward and obstructive. He was 'blasted' for allowing Gerry to walk home alone along the main road and for sending her into school with no lunch when she was ill. Everyone at that meeting agreed that Gerry needed help for the 'emotional trauma' that she had suffered. Henry would not agree to that and would not agree to school contacting me if she were ill again. We did not get round to the photographs but I was assured that they would be attached to my statement and be produced in court.

The meeting finished at 11.30am and my health visitor said that social services would deem Henry's behaviour as 'emotional abuse' and that Gerry would get the help that she needed.

I was in court again on Friday 9th December (another different barrister); once he had established my story with the head teacher, etc., he wanted the hearing postponed until he had the minutes of the Child in Need meeting. Even the idiot man from CAFCASS was now concerned.

Quote from my diary at that time:- "It is such a relief to know that after 2 years people are finally beginning to realise what Henry is really like."

I was very brave and went on a holiday (on my own) to Tunisia 14th December - 21st December. Gerry visited on 24th December for lunch and came to the Christingle service with me.

2006

Gerry wanted to have her ears pierced and I said that I would take her. Henry went mad and said that if I took her 'I would find out what he could really do to me'. I told him that there was nothing left that he could do to me!

The phone calls were not going well as Gerry was either silly or nasty with me. This was obviously very upsetting and I did have many talks with the vicar about it. Henry had turned Ben against me and was trying to do the same with Gerry. I even phoned a psychic help line and was told that 'the tables will turn'; the 'psychic' also told me that Henry is lonely and scared; she didn't see Gerry staying with Henry and that I may move house soon; she even forecast a new man for me! I was not terribly impressed with that news; I had absolutely no intentions of getting involved with another man after what Henry had put me through.

There was a review of the last 'Child in Need' meeting at Gerry's school at 1.30pm on Wednesday 18th January. Henry hijacked that whole meeting and was shouting at me to 'be quiet' and banging the table. He was also shouting at the Headteacher and wanted a change of venue. I was actually pleased that he behaved in that way as it showed the team what he was really like. He still refused to give his consent for Gerry to have the help she needed.

My work load was building up and I was having treatments at the hospital on my arms: deep friction massage, which really hurt, and ultrasound.

The nurse from Gerry's school phoned to let me know that social services were involved in Gerry's care again as Henry was still being awkward.

I was now finding it difficult to afford the rent as I was working 25 hours a week and as a result my benefits had been stopped. The landlord was very understanding and agreed to me getting someone in to share.

Another life-saving activity at this time was getting involved in a musical. Ian, from church, asked me if I would like to join him and his wife to sing in a choir at another church. They were going to join in with Roger Jones' choir from Birmingham in a performance of 'Jailbreak'. Roger Jones formed CMM (Christian Music Ministries) and has written many musicals. Joining this helped me in so many ways. Gerry would also sing the songs with me when she visited, even though she was still extremely unpleasant to me on the phone.

Thursday 16th February was a most horrendous day due to an incident at work - not Henry. I was visiting one of my clients but she had taken an overdose the previous evening and was dead. The police were most unpleasant and told me that 'As I knew the family, I could tell the daughter'. I do not know how I got through that day. The CPN who had been working with this lady was with me and we supported each other – it was only when we had finished talking with the children and when social services arrived, that we could leave and we both cried. I then had to go to the office – my manager should have come out and taken over from me, so I was upset on many levels and very angry that he left me in that awful situation. I refused to stay at the office to write up my report on the incident and I was back in court the next day to sort out contact issues with Ben and Gerry. I promised my manager that he would have the report on his desk first thing in the morning.

Once home I just sat in my armchair for about an hour before I could bring myself to write up the report. I phoned Gerry and she asked why I sounded so sad.

My vicar drove me to the court in Sale, after dropping my report into the office. After lots of discussion with my solicitor and barrister (yet another different one), I agreed to settle for what contact I had, only because social services were supposed to be back on the case. The barrister was also going to ask the judge to order Henry to agree to the help for Gerry but I said that I wanted that kept out of the court. The judge did however insist that it was stated clearly in the order why I had to do that and she also made the CAFCASS officer speak to the children after school that day to explain to them what had happened. The vicar was appalled at the whole court process. I was back home at 3.30pm and never managed to speak with Gerry as no-one was answering the phone; that was the case the whole weekend. The 'Jailbreak' rehearsal on Sunday evening helped me feel better in myself.

Gerry's visit with me the following Tuesday started off badly, she would only grunt at me until I pointed out my new keyboard. Her attitude changed instantly and she asked to play it. Gerry was having saxophone lessons at school and we would have great fun together playing and singing. When Henry found out, Gerry's lessons suddenly stopped.

I was feeling really bad about the lady that died but I was scared to be referred for counselling, (as my manager had suggested) in case he saw it as a sign of weakness. Gerry's visit the following Saturday was from 11am (Henry made her sit in the car until exactly 11am!) went well; I had bought some headphones for my keyboard and she had a good time singing along to 'Home on the range'.

I went to The Algarve region of Portugal for the first week of March (it was snowing when I left England!); another holiday on my own. Though I was really enjoying my holiday I was still having awful dreams and I was still upset about the lady who had killed herself. In one dream about her, I was told that I'd had enough time to be upset but I argued that you cannot put a time limit on grief.

The day of The Jailbreak performance arrived! Saturday 25th March and Gerry arrived at 11am and we went straight over to Tesco's and bought bananas, grapes, strawberries, three lots of wraps, crisps etc. Ian, his wife and another friend collected me and Gerry at 1pm and were amazed at how much food we had packed. The first performance was at 4pm and it went very well; Roger Jones gathered everyone together just before we went on stage for prayers and blessings. Gerry joined in with this. She then took photos and told me afterwards that 'it wasn't as boring as she thought it would be'! We had our tea around 6pm and Henry collected Gerry at 7pm – it had taken a great deal of effort on my solicitors part to get him to agree to that. The second performance was at 7.30pm and was even better than before. I was on such a 'high' afterwards.

I had a visit from social services at 9am on Wednesday 29th March. They now seem to understand what I have been telling them about Henry, especially since they witnessed his behaviour at the last Child in Need review meeting. They were arranging with the school nurse to start working with Gerry as soon as possible even though Henry had insisted it doesn't start until the end of September – tough! I was asked to call into Gerry's school and spoke with the deputy head. She said that the staff are very concerned about Gerry and told me about an incident that occurred that day. Gerry had thrown her work into the bin, she was sobbing and shaking and said that no-one knows what is happening to her and what she is going through. Her teacher told me that Gerry's work had deteriorated since the beginning of March and that her attitude is awful, she had told her teacher "You can't tell me what to do – I can do what I want". The staff were also worried that Gerry had 'fixated' on a boy in her class. When I related all of this to my Health Visitor, she said that she would speak to Child Protection again. When I did meet with her the following Monday she said that we should just let social services get on with their job and that as they now have to 'backtrack' on their original thinking they were probably feeling rather foolish. I was not really bothered about how they feel – it was Gerry that I was worried about.

On her Tuesday visit with me, Gerry was fine until the last 20 minutes when she did the whole 'Catherine Tate Teenager' routine on me; she was absolutely horrible! I went to the communion service and meeting at church later and came away from that as a member of the PCC (Parochial Church Council)! I thought that I was offering to give out the hymnals and service sheets as people arrived! Still, more nights out for me – monthly meetings at church and August off.

Gerry was with me the day of Ben's 13th birthday – Saturday 8th April. She was 15 minutes late and Henry actually apologised and said he would pick her up at 7.15pm to make up the time. She was in a good mood and we went shopping in town as she wanted to buy some holiday clothes. Ben arrived at 7.15pm to collect her and demanded a card and some money for his birthday. I told him that there was a card and present for him in Gerry's bag and received a thank you – progress! Henry went back to being difficult and refused to talk to me when I wanted to arrange to call round with some bras for Gerry – they were not the sort of thing that he would have thought of buying for her.

When I got home from work the following Monday, there was a message from my solicitor saying that she had received a fax from Henry's solicitors; outlining all sorts of stupid threats I was supposed to have made to him. I managed to speak with her and explained how he had been the previous night.

As I was still finding it a struggle to pay the rent I asked my manager for 30 hours/week. I had been informed that I would receive more money in Tax Credits but would lose it all if I worked full time. How bizarre is that? The whole system is so complex and it is a stupid situation to find that you cannot afford to work full time because you are then penalized via the weird and not so wonderful tax credit system.

My landlord called round to tell me about a one bed flat he was doing up nearby and that I had first refusal. I did drive over to locate the flat and can't say that I was that impressed as it was over his estate agency and opposite a pub and kebab take-away.

The mileage claim system at work was getting me down as well, I could not claim for the first visit of the day and on many occasions I lost out; an example of this was when I went to visit a new referral who lived in a nursing home. I arrived in time for our 10.30am meeting and she told me to go away as she had visitors! I just went home but that meant I couldn't claim the mileage so I was doubly annoyed – the money and my wasted time. I had also been given some very difficult clients to support and was getting more and more stressed.

Tuesday 2nd May proved to be the last day I saw Gerry. I collected her from school at 3.15pm and she was awful to me the whole time – I still have no idea why. I went to my belly dance class the next evening but left early as the pain in my arms was so bad. At 8.30pm I had a visit from a lone policeman who said he was there to arrest me for 'harassing' Henry! Apparently he had complained to the police about my 6.30pm telephone calls to the children. I was incensed and told the police officer to sit down whilst I found the document from court stating that I should call the children at that time each evening unless they were visiting with me. Once he had seen that document, and the two pictures of herself that Gerry had put on my mobile phone, his attitude towards me changed. His 'off the record' advice was to record the conversations with Henry.

One of my friends, who I had actually met on the psychiatric ward whilst in hospital (and had helped me get started with embroidery), had taken very ill again mentally and had been sectioned; she then had three heart attacks on the ward.

When I phoned the children on the Friday I had to leave a message. Henry rang back at 7.20pm and said that there had been 'new developments' and that I could not phone or see Gerry – she was due to be with me all day Saturday. He said that his solicitor had been in touch with my solicitor during the day. I felt that this was total rubbish. I would have had a message from my solicitors if what he had said was true.

That was when something in me flipped; I phoned a friend from church and she told me to go straight round. She had also phoned the vicar and he went round as well. Even the vicar described Henry as 'an evil bastard'. Her husband drove me back home at 10pm. I tried to go to bed but ended up cleaning, filing, etc., and I mowed the back lawn at 8.30am. I wanted to leave everything neat and tidy and just vanish. However, my friend phoned and came over. When she saw the state I was in she called my surgery and then A&E at the hospital. Her husband drove us over and after an initial talk with the emergency GP I had to wait over three hours to see the duty psychiatrist. He was very kind and understanding; he wanted to admit me but as there was no bed available, he arranged for the crisis team to see me. One of the team was a nurse I knew from my six months on the ward. He said that someone would phone me in the morning to let me know what time they would visit and that I should try to carry on as 'normal'.

Margaret was given three sleeping tablets for me which I took about 9pm, however, I was up at 2.30am carrying on sorting and tidying. My friend got up with me for a while and persuaded me to go back to bed. As soon as I could I was back up and busy; I took her a drink up at 7.45am and her husband collected us at 9am for church. She was reading, her husband was on duty and I was singing. It was an ordeal trying to get through the hymns; I was shaking so much that the lady next to me had to hold my music for me.

At the end of the service I just collapsed into a sobbing, pathetic heap and was eventually taken home. The crisis team didn't get to me until 5pm and I was worried about work so I phoned the on call number. I gave my rota for the coming week and highlighted the visits which worried me. I was advised to self-certify and stay off on sick leave for the week.

When the CPN arrived, he spent some time talking with me and stared in disbelief at my account of the abuse I had received from Henry. He agreed that I needed to be admitted and he arranged for a bed for me at the hospital. I quickly got a bag together, with my friends' help and the CPN drove me to the hospital. He accompanied me to the ward and stayed with me until the psychiatrist arrived. I was given one Zopiclone and two tranquillisers and slept from about 11pm to 6am.

The next day I phoned my DV support worker and she arranged to visit me on Tuesday morning. The psychiatrist I had been seeing, had just left a few weeks earlier but I recognised many other members of staff. I was given the same medication as the previous night and slept until 6am. My DV support worker visited as promised and told me that she had spoken with the domestic violence unit. The police officer who had visited me about the 'harassing' phone calls had been in touch with them as well; he believed me and told them that it was Henry doing the harassing, not me. My vicar and some other friends from church came to see me in the evening.

My time during the day was spent in the non-smoking lounge listening to Radio 3 – I found it a very good way of deterring other people! Two other ladies used to join me; they were OK, we were the 'sane' nutters! The psychiatrist, who looked about 16 years old, agreed with me that I didn't need medication and said that he thought I was 'just' suffering from extreme stress.

My solicitor told me that I would have to go back to the courts about contact with the children....if I really wanted to.

The staff on psychiatric wards seem to work on the premise that if you are not weeping and wailing all over the place, and are not causing any fuss, then you must be OK. They didn't seem to have noticed, that I had put all the videos and paperbacks into alphabetical order and the hardbacks in size order. They also had no idea of the desperate struggle going on in my mind: whether I should allow myself to live and continue suffering, or kill myself and let someone else suffer for a change. Those thoughts may seem very selfish to others reading this; however, those are the words I wrote in my journal at the time and expressed what I was feeling then. I was living in a nightmare and had no idea how to get out.

When my DV support worker visited again we discussed various options and came up with a four sided plan:- three for the children and one for Henry.

1) Go back to court; I probably wouldn't have got the contact back but it would have really pissed him off and cost him money. It may have also pointed out the fact that I was (and still am) the children's mother and that I will always have parental responsibility.
2) Kick Social Services into action with 'Child in Need meetings' and push for the emotional help for Gerry.
3) Use Family Liaison to work with Gerry (and Ben?) when she moves up to High School in September.
4) Arrange an interview with the police and put in a complaint of harassment against Henry, also to stop him sending the police out and wasting their time.

Because we discussed all the above, my support worker thought that 'Boudica' was back on her chariot! Whilst I was with her a card was delivered to me from another friend at church with a really appropriate verse inside. I was still managing on just the sleeping tablet and was still getting very vivid and weird dreams – no change there then! I found the mornings the most difficult to cope with as I knew that I had another day to get through without my children and I just didn't see the point. I still have difficulties with that. I could feel my 'bubble' forming round me again. The questionnaires given to me by the staff did not ask how you coped with each day. Most of the time I could put on the 'jolly, dotty, Lynne' routine but inside I was being torn apart.

Some friends from church took my sick note into work; I was really worried about losing my job; who would want an unstable, stressed out support worker?

On the Sunday I walked down to the chapel for the 11am service and became very upset. The minister was saying that 'Jesus is always with you when you need him'! I thought, well I must have been overlooked as usual; if I am having to suffer like this it must be for a reason, therefore I must have done something at sometime, that was really awful. In my reasoning at that time it meant that my support worker and friends were all wrong about me, therefore I did not deserve my children, therefore I did not deserve to live.

On Monday 15th May I wrote the following:-

"I really struggled to get through yesterday. The lady who took the service walked me back to the ward – I asked her to, as I was so upset and could easily have walked out. A nurse let me in and asked how I was – I told him that I had written everything down – he said that I should show my writings to a doctor.

The day just got worse and worse and eventually (late evening) another nurse took me to my room to talk; I couldn't, so I showed her what I had written. Her response was that I should always tell the staff exactly how I was feeling – I did not feel able to do that as 'it's only me' and I'm supposed to be able to sort things out for myself.

Some friends from church did visit me and did their very best to cheer me up.

The next day I had an appointment at another hospital about my elbows and was told that I had tennis elbow in my right arm and golfer's elbow in my left arm. He asked if I had any hobbies and when I told him that I went swimming, dancing, and singing, he said 'Anything useful?' I was very upset at that and asked the psychiatric nurse, who had taken me to come in to the consulting room with me. The consultant then said that he would refer me for physiotherapy (I had already had seven sessions but they had 'lost' my notes). The nurse with me was very good and very understanding, after the appointment he took me shopping and then back to my house so I could water my plants, collect my post and a change of clothes. He even turned the engine over on my car and then he drove us to his church he showed me round and bought us coffee. He also gave me a big hug when we got back to the ward and told me that I would be OK.

I was discharged on 17th May, a friend from church took me home and suggested that I mow the lawns – I did. I didn't get to speak with Gerry until the following Sunday and she was pleasant. That changed completely the next day when I phoned – she was very rude and refused to ever visit me.

The main boss from The Agency visited me during the week, to discuss work and told me that the counselling she was offering through work was only to discuss 'work issues'. How do you separate issues? She seemed to think that I had a problem with men; she was wrong, I have a problem with 'mega-prats'! I returned to work on 5th June.

The phone calls to the children were either not answered or answered very rudely; I was then informed one day that the children were away with Henry in Norfolk for two weeks – he hadn't let me know.

I somehow managed to get through work on 15th June but in the evening I 'lost it'. I wrote that I phoned the on-call number at work and told the lady that I had taken all my tablets. She told me to unlock the front door whilst she phoned an ambulance; she kept me talking until they came. During the night on the ward a man was admitted to the ward and put in the bed opposite me, I was convinced that it was Henry and insisted that the nurse check for me. She assured me that it was not him but he had similar clothes to the ones which Henry wore and had the same mannerisms; he even awarded the nurse a 'gold star' for the injection she gave – very like Henry. Luckily he was moved to a different ward; I was watching the clock most of the night and it was going backwards!

I was discharged on Saturday, 17th June after a great deal of bargaining. The staff were having a great deal of trouble understanding the fact that as Henry was working as a counsellor at the hospital I could not remain on the ward and be in their system.

I was back in court on Monday, 26th June and the barrister (again another one) was brilliant. As I was not in a good state mentally, he arranged that I did not have to see Henry or the judge. He also assured me that he would make sure that I got enough money in my settlement to buy a house locally. Famous last words! I was meant to be seeing a friend in the village that evening but it didn't quite work out. I (apparently) took all of my tablets, texted a friend to tell him that I didn't need a lift and that my will was on the dining table. For some unknown (to me) reason my next door neighbour called round to see me and called an ambulance.

I was back home the next day and my vicar came to see me; he was very angry with me and seemed to think, that because people had done their best to help me that I should be fine. It doesn't work like that, at least not for me, and we had a big argument about it. My GP referred me back to the crisis team and two of the team came out to me near the end of the week. One of the women was patronising and condescending and had obviously not read my notes; she said she understood how hard things were for me because I don't make friends easily! The team visited me every day and sometimes twice a day as they were bringing out the medication I needed. (They had decided that it was safer not to leave that with me).

My counselling sessions, which had been arranged from work, started on Monday 10th July and were in an area I was not familiar with, so some friends from church drove the route with me the evening before. One of those same friends also came with me to the next 'Child in Need meeting' on Monday 17th July, but Henry wouldn't let her into the room. So, those present were:- myself, a representative from social services, the head of safe-guarding children (ha-ha), my health visitor and the nurse from Ben's school. The headmistress should have been there as well but didn't make it.

At that meeting Henry was told that 'Gerry needs her mother' to which he replied "No, she just needs a woman". He was also told that contact should be set up again, as per the court order and that he (Henry) should actively promote that. He agreed to that in the meeting. The meeting finished just before 11am – after Henry had told the meeting that he had to have police patrolling the house because he 'lived in fear for his life'! When I recounted that fact to my DV support worker she just laughed; at that time I was manically driving all over the UK – I would drive to Wales, Cromer, Whitby, in fact anywhere that I could – many times in the middle of the night, so, if the police were following me they must have had a good tour of the UK!

The last visit from the crisis team was on Friday 4th August, my weight had gone down to 9st 3lbs and I was looking a lot better – physically anyway! The CPN was not happy though, and said that he would write to my GP recommending that I would benefit from one to one help. I was told that I could still call the crisis team if necessary.

I had encountered great difficulties when trying to speak with Gerry, the times I did speak with her were not pleasant – as suggested earlier, I recorded those conversations; my DV support worker said that you could almost feel Henry's presence.

All during that time I was swimming every morning (7.30am) and managed between 30 and 60 lengths. I am sure that helped with losing all the weight and was also making me feel better in myself. I was back on Mirtazapine but was only given 14 days supply at a time, that meant that I was seeing my GP every couple of weeks and he was extremely good with me.

I had phoned in an attempt to speak with Gerry, but she was so awful and I kept playing the recording of the 'conversation' over and over again, that was all I could remember of that evening.

On Sunday 13th August I woke up but could not understand why I couldn't get out of bed; I was in hospital in a bed in A&E attached to various monitors. After a talk with the duty psychiatrist I was told that I could go home – how? I was in my nightie. One friend I phoned was still in work and so I phoned Ian and he came over for me. I was lying asleep on chairs in the corridor when he arrived and he had brought his ex-wife's coat with him. He took me home and stayed with me whilst I had a shower and got dressed – I was still falling over. He made us both a drink and told me that I had to make a difficult decision - I either keep phoning Gerry and destroying myself, or accept the fact that I had done everything I possibly could to let the children know that I am there for them and get on with my own life. He said that he would pick me up at 7pm for the Jailbreak rehearsal. That went very well and when I was back home (9.30pm) I decided to phone the crisis team to try to find out what had happened the previous night.

Unfortunately it was the CPN that I found to be very insensitive who answered; she said that I had called the crisis team for help but had to leave a message; by the time they called back I had taken all the tablets so they called an ambulance and got me to open the front doors. She then told me that I had refused to co-operate with and was abusive with the paramedics – 'very bad behaviour Lynne'. They waited until the tablets knocked me out and then took me to hospital. I did not have any recollection of that, which is what I found really scary.

I was back seeing psychiatrists but they changed every couple of weeks as they were only given very short contracts - what good does that do the patients? At the same time I also had no choice but to move into the flat that my landlord had done up for me; that upset me so much as it meant that there was absolutely no chance of the children ever coming to stay with me – it was only a one bedroomed flat. Other people did not seem to understand the significance of that, but to me it meant that Henry had won. I was devastated. I managed to get my landlord to agree to me painting my bedroom pink!

The OT (Occupational Therapist) explained to me that my 'lost periods of time' were 'dissociative episodes' and I used to have some quite difficult sessions with her.

On Tuesday 12th September my landlord arrived at 9.30am (I had already had my swim of 30 lengths that morning). He started to move my furniture into the new flat; I thought that he was over to make arrangements for the move! I phoned a friend and she came straight over to help me pack up and I excused myself from the PCC meeting that evening. The move took two days in total and my eldest son came the next evening to assemble my bed for me.

The next couple of weeks were taken up with settling into the flat, i.e., painting, cleaning and rehearsals for Jailbreak; the performance was on 1st October and I impressed many people. My 'counselling' sessions were to end on 9th October and were not exactly successful.

Some friends from church took me to my hospital appointment on 17th October – I had been having 'female' problems and was booked in for an operation – once my BP was lowered. It was 187/120 at that time and too high! The lady consultant had received a detailed letter from my GP and assured me that she would not examine me; I needed a hysteroscopy under general anaesthetic.

The next day I was back in court where it became apparent that Henry had 'lost' £50K – he would not account for that money. He also said that he was off sick with 'stress' so his income had dropped from over £30K/year to £19K/year. One estate agency had faxed through their valuation of the house to be £450K (as opposed to £285K from the agency Henry had used). Yet Henry still had the nerve to tell the judge that they were a dubious firm! The judge was not impressed and Henry was ordered to account for the missing £50K and was also told that he must sell the house. However, as Henry had the children living with him he could be re-housed and I was left out in the cold as 'there just isn't enough money in the pot for me to buy a house'. Isn't it funny how the story alters – first I was told that I would get enough money to buy myself a cottage and then I couldn't – Henry was still adamant that I would not receive a penny.

My friends from church who were with me at court were brilliant, they took me out when court was over for lunch and then we went to another little country church.

Christian Retreat

I had been persuaded by other members of my church to attend a four day Christian Retreat; it was led by Ian (who is now my husband), so that day I had to get three days zooming in before being trapped!

I arrived in the evening and there were plenty of people to guide me up the drive, someone took my case up to my room – sorry, cell - just room for a single bed and no en-suite! I sent a one word text message to Tim (a friend from church) which said 'help' – he replied 'You can do it'. I put up the 'Footprints' picture which he and his wife had given me and went for tea at 6.30pm. That was an ordeal and I threw up after it. I was then told by Ian that we all had to be silent until after morning Eucharist! I told him that he must have one more screw loose than I thought.

There were just 8 participants and about 6 million staff; we were split into 2 tables – St Chad (mine) and St Cedd. I did know some of the people from Jailbreak. Each day consisted of 5 talks and a couple of meditations and if we were really lucky – 'artwork'!

I was getting worse by the minute – I was physically sick and was shaking – I left the house and sat under a tree for a while and then went to my room and lay on my bed. I spoke to my friend from church and he said that he wouldn't think any less of me if I didn't stay but I promised him that I would give it my best shot.

Ian's then wife, brought one of the vicars to me and I explained a little of my history to her. She said that I was a 'torture' victim and was suffering from 'Post Traumatic Stress' and that I could recover. She also said that as I was convinced I was going to die 'Why didn't I just enjoy the time I had left?'

The weekend actually turned out to be quite good fun – I incorporated 'chaos theory' into my art work and Ian's group made up a song dedicated to me about a 14' spider! There is a story behind the spider. Not long after I had moved into the flat I found a huge (14') spider on the carpet in my bedroom; nobody would leave work to come and sort it out for me and so I asked the girls in the office below me, they said that I had to learn to do that for myself as it is 'character building'! The next day Ian told me that he had seen my 14' 'beast' up by a farm and that it looked a 'friendly fellow' – the farmer had put 'legs' on hay bales so that it looked very much like a spider.

Each meal time we had to sit where our names were so that you always sat with someone new to you; there were place mats which we turned over at the end of the meal and one of mine said 'Lord, last night I prayed for patience – what's the hold up?' I was convinced that was a set up but Ian insists otherwise.

A very special surprise was on the Sunday morning when our friends and supporters from our churches came to join us at morning prayer.

That weekend gave me the strength to carry on and face the next set of meetings. I went (along with a couple of friends from church) to the 'Child in Need meeting' on 1st November to be told that they had no record of a meeting. It had been rescheduled to the 3rd November at 12 noon but no-one had thought to inform me.

That meeting never happened and I was really losing the plot; strange things would happen in my flat – objects being moved, etc., which I found very scary – I was convinced that I had a ghost. I was even eating in my sleep.

I told all of that to my DV support worker and she said, that as I was starving myself during the day I was eating at night. I would get up in the mornings to find a plate of cheese and biscuits in the microwave, the shower gel on the settee and clothes spread out over the furniture in the living room. My CPN put these 'incidents' down to 'dissociative behaviour', I think it was more likely to be the medication that I had been put on.

I was still seeing my GP regularly and because I had suddenly started bleeding again after 5 years. I had to have an investigation under anaesthetic; it was also decided that the smear test would be done at the same time (I had avoided them as I was too afraid of experiencing more pain because of Henry's attacks). My friend Tim took me into hospital on the morning of 10th November; he collected me at 7am, I was in theatre at 9.25am and sitting up with a hot drink at 11.30am! He took me home and got on with painting the doors in my flat whilst I went to bed and slept (I had had a general anaesthetic so was still a bit groggy). His wife, Yvonne, arrived when she had finished work and we had a take away for tea. She stayed the night with me and her husband went back home – I only had a one bedroom flat and so she took the sofa. The reason for mentioning this episode is because when I went back to my GP for the results, the consultant had written that I still had 'an internal healing area' where Henry had damaged me.

My DV support worker told me that she would be withdrawing her support after the next court case, but that I could still phone if I needed her. She had been working with me for three years when the limit is usually two – but I was a special case! She said that I had done really well – my weight was now down to 8st 12lbs and I felt great about that.

The next meeting with my barrister was due to be

Monday 29th November, but it was cancelled because she had not received all the relevant financial information from Henry's solicitors, especially the valuation on the house. Henry was extremely obstructive about that, not allowing the estate agent into the house until ordered to and then only allowing him to see certain rooms.

I had my final meeting with the OT (Occupational Therapy – more of a counselling session) on 23rd November and on my return drive I had a phone call from my solicitor, asking why I hadn't turned up for the meeting with the barrister! The answer was quite simple – I didn't know about it – they had written, not phoned, and sent the letter to the wrong address!

CMM came to my rescue again as I went on one of Roger Jones' music weeks at Crowhurst, near Eastbourne. The theme for the week was Jailbreak so I knew the songs very well and in fact managed to sing nearly every female part. I coped very well with the music part of the week but I found the worship and talks sessions very painful. I felt, and still feel, very guilty that Ben and Gerry are still with Henry while I managed to escape; then I felt guilty about actually enjoying the singing. The music weeks run by CMM are well worth going on and can be very healing, I strongly recommend them. I received many supportive text messages during that week from other church friends.

The next court case was on 7th December and I had a meeting with my DV support worker two days prior to that. She explained that I would probably feel very strange when the court cases are all over – it had taken three years – and she wanted me to be prepared emotionally.

I went before the judge (with my solicitor and barrister)

at 2.20pm to be cross-examined; that didn't take very long. Henry's cross-examination was at 3pm and the judge had to call a halt at 4.30pm as the court was closing. During the proceedings I caught Henry glaring at me (he was sat right opposite me), I looked him straight back in his eyes and he turned away – a victory of some sort! My barrister had tied Henry in all sorts of knots over his finances and it was wonderful to see him squirm. We were back in court the next morning at 9.45 and my barrister continued to cross-examine Henry. The judge called everyone back into court at 2pm; he said that he wasn't impressed with Henry's attempts to first maximise the amount of money needed to do up the house (£89K) and then to minimise it under cross-examination (£15K).

The final decision was that the judge split the valuation, a ridiculously low £285K, 70/30. That meant that Henry had to pay me £86,550 by 26th January 2007 or sell the house. He was furious and I just wanted to get out as quickly as possible.

While all these court proceedings were going on I had been trying to get help from CAB (Citizens advice Bureau) about Incapacity Benefit, Income Support and DLA (Disability Living Allowance). I was seeing my GP very regularly, weekly as he was still only giving me short supplies of my much reduced medication.

One Saturday I was having a mega-baking session for church and Ian kept texting me - I misunderstood his last message to me which said 'Text interruptions can be a pain in the neck'; I thought that he was angry with me and so I cut my wrist several times with a serrated knife. I text'd back that my baking session was over but I seemed to have cut myself; Ian and his wife came straight over and spent most of the rest of the day with me.

The stress of three years of court appearances and my children's behaviour towards me, had a very negative effect on me and it was obvious to people that I was not coping well. That Christmas was spent with the family of my good friends at church, who helped me so much throughout all that time.

I invited some friends from church for a meal on 30th December and they said that they were praying that Henry didn't pay me the money, as I could then get 43% of the value of the house and would therefore be much better off.

The next day was spent writing letters to social services, my GP, my health visitor, my psychiatrist and to MP's; I was desperate to get some help and was reaching out to anyone I could think of. I had already tried my local MP and was then writing to Anne Widdicombe and Sir Nicholas Winterton.

Ms Widdicombe's secretary replied saying that she was unable to become involved and Sir Nicholas did at least write to social services but reached another stone wall.

2007

Ian, along with another friend from church, had helped me with those letters. I was much more open about what Henry had actually done to me and when I spoke with my GP he assured me that he would back me up with my medical records. He also said that he himself was fed-up, with being ignored by social services whenever he voiced his concerns over the welfare of Ben and Gerry.

I felt awful after I had delivered and posted all of the letters as I felt totally raw, open, exposed and extremely vulnerable. I was terrified of what Henry might do to the children as he knew, and still knows, that hurting the children would hurt me the most.

On January 3rd I wrote in my journal:-

"Feel awful – really frightened – want to vanish. Managed to get all of my tablets off Ian. It seems so much more shameful with everything in writing. I am not safe and neither are the children – that man is a complete monster.

Just make sure that the children know that I have been fighting for them solidly these last three years. I love them dearly, this is why it hurts so much.

I realise that people are getting fed-up of being around me and I apologise to them for that........

I seem to have torn a page out, I don't really remember what happened apart from Gerry phoning me on my mobile; she was awful and told me that she had smashed the Christmas present I sent her and that I should stop bothering her.

I think it was then that I took all of my tablets – 2 weeks worth"

I was not happy when I woke up the next day. Sometime during the morning Ian's wife phoned me to say, I had sent a text message to Ian at 2am and phoned him at 3am insisting that it was 7am. Ian and his wife came over and insisted that I stay with them for a few days. After a visit to my GP and another to my psychiatrist I was back in the care of the crisis team. That seemed to give me a glimmer of hope regarding the children, as one member of the crisis team said that she would get me an advocate to help sort out social services. She also gave me a care plan (pink) and a pass for the gym and the swimming pool. We made a deal – if I feel that I have to take all of the tablets I must phone the crisis team first and talk to them.

Ian and his wife called round in the evening with a meat and potato pie for me. Ian wanted to put some petrol in my car and I finally had to admit that I had no idea where my car was! I showed them both my care plan and also told them that the team agreed that I really needed someone to talk to about the abuse – but that now was not the right time. Part of my journal entry for that evening read:-

"I had watched a video I recorded some time ago about Angela Channings who was accused of killing 2 of her babies; even she was allowed to see her daughter 3 times per week (under supervision), but at least she saw her. I have done nothing wrong – I just left that evil husband of mine and I haven't seen Ben since September 2005 and Gerry since May 2006. Something is terribly wrong."

I explained to the crisis team that I was struggling with the new tablets (levomepromazine) they made me very ill and totally spaced out – I had no idea what I was doing or saying. I had an appointment with the crisis team's psychiatrist on 16th January; his first question was 'What did I think my diagnosis was?'

I told him in no uncertain terms that I didn't give a damn what he thought my diagnosis was. I told him that I felt awful and that he was to sort it without putting me in a box and labelling me. He then said that I had recovered from this before and what did I think the probability was that I would recover again. I told him that I didn't know but would engage the 'improbability drive' to find out! (Read "The Hitch Hikers Guide to the Galaxy" by Douglas Adams if you don't understand).

The man at the job-centre was really understanding and said that he could offer all sorts of help – even the CBT (Cognitive Behavioural Therapy). This had been recommended by my psychiatrist but I would have had to pay at least £50/hour! A non starter!

A friend from church had transferred the tapes of Gerry's phone conversations with me onto a CD, which I took to my advocate. Another friend from church helped me sort out my papers for the next 'Child in Need' meeting.

The crisis team introduced me to my very own CPN (Community Psychiatric Nurse) – a very young man; I was not impressed. That was the last of the crisis team's involvement.

Escaping The Fear

2008

A miracle happened:- I was divorced from Henry and he had paid up!!!

Now it may seem to people reading this that £86,500 is a lot of money. There was not much of it left by the time I had paid: £30,000 to the building society for the Buxton house (if I had been able to pay it off earlier it would have been only £18,000 but Henry had not given me any of the correspondence relating to that house), £23,500 had to be paid to my solicitors – my legal 'aid' was only a loan. I had three credit cards to pay off and also repay my friends and my eldest son the money they had lent me as well as a small loan I had taken out. The next problem I found was that if anyone has over £6000 then their benefits are stopped. I obviously did not have enough money to buy myself a house (as promised by one barrister), so I had to remain in private rented accommodation. In order to keep my benefits I needed to spend the rest of the money on things that I actually needed and could justify to the benefits agencies. I decided to get a better car, a decent hi-fi system (B&O) and a full size electric piano.

I tried to deposit £10,000 in a different bank than my own and encountered even more discrimination – I was not able to open a new account as I was divorced!

One morning I had arranged to give Ian a lift into work – that felt very strange as he worked in the building next to where I had worked! I also had a couple of test drives arranged at the local garage. I decided on a Toyota Yaris and was even given £200 for my old car.

My last meeting with my DV support worker was on Friday 2nd February; the first thing I said to her was that the drinks were on me as Henry had paid up. She was totally amazed; we were both upset that that was our last meeting and discussed names for my new car – Penelope it was to be.

On Saturday 3rd February I went on another Roger Jones music week, this time at Whitby, called "Precious and Honoured". On Sunday I walked to Robin Hood's Bay and back (8.45am – 4.20pm), about 15 miles.

During that week some more of my settlement money came through and I bought myself a wonderful hooded velvet cape, it was made to measure by a lady who made costumes for films. I also bought myself a cross made out of Whitby Jet. At the end of that week I booked myself on the week for 'A Grain of Mustard Seed' at Grange-over-Sands.

It was during that week that Ian made it quite clear in his text messages how he felt about about me. He said that he would not give up his wife – I knew differently but didn't contradict him. I did talk about this with Roger and another member of his team, who encouraged me to 'pray for his marriage' – I confess that I could not bring myself to do that.

When I was back home I collected my new car. It wasn't until I was going to go on a walk with Ian up Lantern Pike and Kinder Grouse moor, that I realised that I had left my hiking boots at the hotel in Whitby. I did the walk in my trainers and drove back to Whitby the next day with a girl friend from swimming.

My car, Penelope, liked to go to the seaside so we often had trips out – Colwyn Bay, Cromer and Hunstanton; she also liked going to Snowdonia very much!

I was involved in another performance of Jailbreak at my church on Sunday 25th February; I had asked the PCC to help with preparing food for people to share after the performance but they were not agreeable. I told them that I would do that myself then, and I did! Some other people were shamed into helping me – after all, it was to raise money for the church. The performance was a great success and so was I – people said to me 'Knowing how you are, how did you do that?' Ian said it was because they had seen a different side to me that night.

My meetings with my advocates started on 28th February, they were appalled at the treatment I had received from social services and suggested a course of action for me. That involved trying to get a social/support worker to help me with contact with the children, especially Gerry; I had travelled that road before and was not feeling hopeful.

Another disturbing thing was happening to me – I kept seeing Joan (my dead mother) in all sorts of places, at Ian's house in the rocking chair and blocking the doorway of the bedroom I stayed in at his house.

One Saturday I had made a curry meal for Ian and his wife, the vicar and his wife and my other very good friends from church. We had a lovely evening together, but when they had all left I felt awful and cut my wrists again. My logic went like this: how can I be having so much fun and enjoy being with my friends when I know that Ben and Gerry are still trapped in that awful house with that monster? Ian came back with my tablets and made me stay at his house again. He was very angry with me for harming myself again. Two days after that I drove down to Glastonbury and stayed in a Bed and Breakfast called Angel's Place.

I had a message during my time away that another friend of mine, from hospital had died and I went to her funeral on 13th March.

I had decided for some reason to have an aromatherapy session, the lady gave me two very good tips if I felt the need to cut myself; she said to get out a picture of me as a child and imagine that I was her and that I couldn't hurt a little girl. Her second idea was to say in the notes to Gerry that at a specific time each day, is when I am thinking of her especially and Henry can't take that away as he won't know about it. My GP, Ian and a friend from church all thought they were good ideas.

Henry's next door neighbour had told people that she was worried about Gerry and that she would contact social services; she didn't do that as she later said that she was too afraid of Henry.

A letter arrived on 3rd May from social services telling me that someone would carry out an 'initial assessment'. How could it be 'initial' when they have had the case for so long?

A chance meeting with a friend led to me joining a Methodist house group which meets every Tuesday morning. Those people are true Christians and have helped me so much.

A rather upsetting incident occurred when Ben's school nurse said that she would not deliver cards and letters to the children, as they didn't like being pulled out of class to receive them. I was furious and sent her a letter saying that I would continue to do so, as agreed in the last meeting and that it was up to school to find a way of getting the cards and letters to the children. I told Ian about this and he helped me write another letter to social services, MP's, etc., and also told me how tough the fight was going to be. I was obviously upset and when his wife said 'Don't you want to fight for your children?', I could have hit her. I just swore at her and Ian told her to be quiet. How can people be so insensitive? She had also booked herself onto the same music week that I was attending, it was the musical at Grange over Sands. This meant that I had to take her there. However, I got a chest infection and had to leave part way through the week; I couldn't sing so there wasn't much point being on a music week!

That is the end of my journal input, now I have to sort my thoughts out!

Despite the help of the advocates I was no further on

regarding contact with Ben and Gerry and all I could do was write to them and deliver those letters in person to school. I could not trust that they would receive the letters if they were delivered by Royal Mail. Henry did not check the post for days or even weeks and even then, there would be no guarantee that he would give the letters to the children – he never gave me my post when I was in hospital for six months.

So that is what I am left with; delivering letters/cards to Ben and Gerry via school to ensure that they received them.

I was distraught; do I go on harming myself or try to get my life back on track?

Ian gave me the strength to survive, it also helped when in April 2008 I moved out of the flat into a two bedroomed cottage. That was a turning point in my life, I stopped harming myself (overdoses/cutting) and concentrated on making a lovely home. I was off all medication and no longer seeing a psychiatrist or the crisis team.

So what had changed?

The Methodist Tuesday meetings – the people were so supportive and non-judgemental and also the CBT (Cognitive Behavioural Therapy) that I received from the Job Centre.

CBT is so different from counselling, you have to be serious about it and it is hard work. Ian and a lady from the Methodist group really supported and helped me with this.

Escaping The Fear

Cognitive Behavioural Therapy (CBT)

I obviously have many issues, complaints and recommendations after my experiences detailed previously. However, before I tackle those I want to explain how the process of CBT worked and actually helped me. The 'work sheets', for want of a better word, are in the appendices as I am certain that they could be of use to people. I do urge though, not to try to work through them on your own; you really do need a well qualified mentor in that field and a trusted friend/partner to help you along the way.

My first session with my CBT therapist was just outlining what had happened to me in my life, i.e., my mother's treatment of me and also Henry's treatment towards me. A previous counsellor had told me that 'I had completely perplexed her and that she had no idea where to start'. I told that to Becky and she said 'that is rubbish', you only have one problem and that is how you think/feel about yourself. She agreed that, yes, that was due to how I had been treated, but she said that she could give me a way of altering my thinking and change how I reacted to situations.

I was amazed at what she had told me and came out of that meeting with hope. I must admit though, that once I began the 'work' I was wishing that I hadn't started. The first 'assignment' if you want to give these tasks a name, was to write a 'narrative'. That really meant writing a summary of all that had happened to me – not an easy task and so I just started from when Henry and I got together. That was then discussed – in great detail - at the next meeting. My next task was to fill in a 'trauma trigger record' i.e., anything that spooked you out! Next came the 'thought record', take a situation and examine your thoughts. The most difficult task was kept until last and Becky was given permission to spend extra time with me. I had to pick a traumatic incident and write about it, giving as much detail as I could at that time.

I decided to write about the 'incident' that resulted in Gerry. As Becky knew it would be difficult she suggested that I write a little and then take 'time out'. My first attempt took 6 separate inputs. I then had to read those 'inputs' to Becky; we would discuss them, a detailed analysis would follow and my next task was to write in more depth about the same 'incident'. This process continued until I could not add anything more. Then came the hard work! I had to keep reading that text (either on my own or with an understanding friend) until it no longer made me cry. I did challenge Becky on this as I was worried that she was trying to make me 'unfeeling', but she explained that none of what was done to me was my fault and that I could not have stopped it. I could not have got through that without the love and help given to me from Ian and Mabel from the Methodist house group.

When I questioned Mabel about my experiences and especially those of the lady in Austria (whose father had imprisoned and abused her), she just said that 'Nobody said it would be easy' and that I should put my concerns 'At the foot of the cross'. I didn't know how to do that then and I still don't know now.

I did eventually get to the stage where I could read my full narrative to myself and not fall apart. That took an awful long time and I cannot express my gratitude enough to Mabel and Ian for getting me through that time.

Voluntary work at church.

I have mentioned that I became very involved at church; I was a member of the PCC, a sides-person, a cleaner, a member of the singing group and I had also taken on the role of Safety Officer. I felt able to take on those roles, gradually, due to the help I was receiving from my DV Support worker, my CPN and most of all from my friends. The involvement with the church also helped me grow in confidence as had the CBT.

The most challenging role was that of Safety Officer. There were changes in the Health and Safety Regulations applying to churches and as I was an experienced Nuclear Safety Engineer I took on the role. However, I am not convinced that the church really wanted a 'proper' safety officer, as I was constantly obstructed and had to bring in the Fire Officer on many occasions:- as far as I know there has still not been a fire drill at the church! The vicar at the time told me not to have a fire drill during the service! I said 'OK, I will ask the fire to wait outside until the service has finished!'

I don't resent the time I spent on that work – many hours, which must have saved the church a great deal of money as I didn't charge for my time. I really enjoyed doing the work and thought that I was helping the church; however, it appeared that the church did not agree. I was placed in a very difficult situation so I resigned my position as Safety Officer and PCC member and left that church. I also did a sponsored walk to raise funds for the church:- I walked The West Highland Way (Milngavie to Fort William), 95 miles all on my own and raised £800 – my parting gift! There was also another reason for my departure – which will become apparent in the next chapter.

I started to attend the services at the Methodist Church, initially in the community centre as the old church was being knocked down. Ian and I attended the opening service for the new church and we also got married there on 18th September 2010.

I love the uncertainty of Methodist services over the set liturgies of the Anglican and Roman Catholic services and I also love singing; worship is meant to be joyous so let us have joyous songs. Ian and I both feel the same about that. Our way of worship is to help people and to praise God via our music; music is very important to us, I believe that it connects us directly to God, that is my feeling.

Developments with Ian

It will have become apparent by now, that Ian and I were becoming very close and we wanted to be with each other but he was adamant that this was impossible. However, because of his religious and moral views he was in torment about our relationship.

Matters came to a head in October 2008. Ian visited me on Friday 17th and said that he thought, but couldn't promise that he could spend Saturday with me, and put up the shelves in my computer room. However, his text message to me at 21.27 said that arrangements were not working out as he had hoped and so he could not see me; he apologised for 'hurting me in so many ways'. I was obviously upset and disappointed about this but was quite used to being let down at the last moment. He sent me more apologetic messages the next day. I was not at all happy about the way things had deteriorated and told him to 'get it sorted'; he said he couldn't as it was too complicated and too difficult.

The following Sunday afternoon I sent him a text message; I was worried because I hadn't heard from him all day and that was not normal. He replied saying that he was sorry for the lack of contact but that he had gone to church. I carried on wrapping the shoe-boxes for Operation Christmas Child; I had wrapped 40 and just had 70 left! Around 2pm I received another message from him, saying that he had told his wife about us and that our affair had to end. I just slumped into a chair and phoned one of my friends. She came straight over and watched me as I carried on furiously wrapping the rest of the shoe-boxes. She said that his messages didn't make sense, that it wasn't like Ian and that he would be back. She was absolutely correct – though I didn't know it at the time.

There were more text messages and a telephone

conversation at 9.30pm. We arranged to meet the next day (Monday) after work as he was collecting one of his sons from the bus station at 7pm. We had a couple of hours together and it was clear that he was not going to give me up – we just didn't know how things were going to work out.

I should have known that everything would be OK from the chorus of my song when I was playing the part of Lydia in Jailbreak – 'Hope in God, Trust in Him'.

Just after 11pm that night I received another message from Ian, telling me that his wife understood why he could no longer be with her and that she also understood that I was his 'rock' and not the 'wicked witch'. Even so I did not sleep very well that night and waited eagerly for his usual phone call at 6.30am (We always spoke with each other while he was travelling to work). He asked if he could stay with me that night and said that he wanted to visit his mum and his sister after work first. I was on pins the whole time, until he phoned to say he was on his way to me.

I was very surprised when he told me of their reaction to his news; his sister had said 'About time too' and his mum said 'What took you so long? I expected this 30 years ago!' Ian was even more taken aback at his mum's reaction to the news that he had been having an affair with me – she had just said 'Good!'

When he arrived he spoke with his sister and suddenly handed me the phone saying that she wanted to speak with me; I was panic stricken but she was lovely with me and asked if I was looking after her brother – I promised her that I was doing my best.

He was in no state to go into work the next day and when he explained the situation to his boss he was told to take the rest of the week off. That week proved to be very emotional all round; he would often be in floods of tears and I didn't know what to do for the best or what to say. I therefore did the only thing possible – love him, hold him and say nothing.

We arranged to see one of the members of the church singing group later that afternoon so that Ian could explain the situation before the jungle drums exploded. He was very good with us – no comments or criticism – and he said that he would make an announcement at the rehearsal on Thursday that Ian and his wife had decided to separate and that it was amicable (well, as amicable as these things can be).

Mabel and her husband (from the Methodist Tuesday morning group) were another source of emotional help for us both. They were totally non-judgemental.

On the Friday I was taken to meet his mum. My stomach was doing double somersaults as we approached her house, but I was greeted with hugs and thanks for 'looking after Ian'. His sister then arrived closely followed by her husband, so more hugs and kisses! The whole situation was totally bizarre – like a scene from a sitcom.

It was arranged that Ian would stay at his mum's house during the week except, Wednesday as that was when he had his guitar lesson and we also decided to try a local singing group.

Even though Ian had left his house he insisted on returning to finish the decorating he had started – I wasn't happy with that at all and became very anxious every time until he returned to me. We were both in a very emotional state.

The only person (at that time) who was not at all understanding was the vicar, he actually excluded me from his prayers and gave Ian an ultimatum – chose the church or Lynne! Ian's response was 'You have just lost your guitarist!' From then on Ian attended the Methodist church with me and he arranged to meet the minister to talk with him about our situation. The minister had a much more adult approach to our situation and said that while he could not condone our relationship, he could understand it.

We were therefore both accepted into the Methodist Church and enjoyed attending the Tuesday morning group.

Reunion with Ron

Every Christmas time I would send out cards to all my relatives for whom I had addresses. I thought (but may have been mistaken) that I had always put in my current contact details. Christmas 2008 was no exception and was also my first Christmas with Ian. (Christmas 2007 I went on a retreat so that I would not be alone).

I was very surprised one day in January 2009 when I had a telephone call from one of my aunts in Barrow; she had received the card that I'd sent – it seemed that all of the others had not got to her nor to my other relatives. I asked her if she knew where Ron was but she only had the address in St Albans. However, she suggested that I contact another Uncle and Aunt who lived in Windsor. I wrote to them explaining what had happened and then just had to wait – not one of my favourite words!

One day in February 2009, Ian called me to pick up the phone as my brother, John wanted to speak with me. I can remember saying "Yeah, right!" Ian was most insistent and I had my first conversation with John for about 16 years. He promised to e-mail the details of where Ron was living and urged me to get in touch with him. So, one Thursday whilst Ian was at work, I called the home in Wokingham and asked to speak with Ron; the voice on the phone said "Speaking!" I was amazed, I thought that I would be talking to someone on the reception desk, not my dad. I told him that I had been looking for him for so many years because the home in St Albans would not tell me where he had moved to. He said that he had also been searching for me and had finally given up all hope of ever seeing me again. It was an extremely emotional conversation but we managed to make arrangements for myself and Ian to drive down at the weekend to visit him.

Saturday 7th February 2009 was a big day for me and I hope for Ron as well. We were finally reunited and there was no Joan to interfere. We had a long talk and then went out to lunch at Ron's favourite Italian restaurant in Wokingham. Ian took a photograph of Ron and me and that is special.

As we all know, life can be a real sod at times and this proved to be one of those times. Ian worked for Sony Ericsson at their office in Warrington; the company announced that this office was to close at the end of March 2009 but the company offered relocation to Lund in Sweden if anyone was interested. Ian had gone for an interview about the work in Lund and after talking it over with me, he decided to accept the relocation package. That meant that having just found Ron I now had to say goodbye again. During our talks I did ask Ron how he and Joan actually met; that is when he told me the story of how he got me out of care. He gave me a photograph of Joan when she was a young attractive woman and said that I could use it as a dartboard if I wished. I told him how I had walked The West Highland Way on my own for church and he said that I probably did it as I thought Joan was chasing me!

Ian and Ron got on very well and Ron said that it was a good idea to have a fresh start; besides we could always keep in contact via e-mails and SKYPE.

Ian and I had a trip to Lund in March to view a house in a village called Kävlinge, 8 minutes train ride from Lund. It was a detached house with 2 bedrooms and very spacious – a huge kitchen, large study room, enormous living room – which we hardly ever used except when practising our music for church!

Ian's last day of work in Warrington was Tuesday 31st March 2009. The following Thursday we took the ferry from Holyhead to Dublin and drove to Bantry with the intention of walking The Sheep's Head Way. The weather decided otherwise so we only managed to walk a few sections which happened to be the parts that you could not access by car. I can recommend the hotel at Blair's Cove – absolutely stunning views and wonderful accommodation in converted barns, they also run cookery courses.

We took the ferry back from Rosslare to Pembroke and drove to Reading where we stayed in order to have a final visit with Ron before we left for Sweden. That visit with Ron was not uneventful! We went to the same Italian restaurant as before but this time Ron made a dramatic entrance. I held open the glass door to let him in (Ron had no legs and was therefore in an electric wheelchair.) Ron's jacket sleeve caught on the control putting it into top gear and he came hurtling towards me and narrowly missed my toes! He did not however miss colliding with the glass entrance door and smashing into a glass table. The table shattered into innumerable pieces and Ron was stuck in his wheelchair. The mechanism had jammed and it took a waiter and Ian nearly 15 minutes to free it.

Unfortunately, the gear was now stuck in 'fast mode' and I can still see the looks of terror on other diners' faces, as Ron hurtled through the restaurant before coming to a halt at our table! He called the manageress over and offered to make recompense but she refused – he was a well respected customer after all. After a good meal and an emotional farewell Ian and I set off back home to prepare for our move to Sweden on Thursday 16th April. We did have a farewell meal with family and our friends at a very good Indian restaurant before we left.

Escaping The Fear

Life in Sweden

This can be summed up in one simple word:- **UNBEARABLE!**

Maybe I should elaborate slightly on that, maybe not; I think that I could write another book on my experiences and thoughts on living in Sweden. To explore that area in this book would be straying off the point. I am trying to get over to people the controlling nature of my ex-husband and further evidence will be revealed in this chapter.

A summary of our life in Sweden is that Ian went to work during the week at Sony Ericsson and during that time I endured 10 hours of solitary confinement. I do not like to be idle, so I busied myself in the garden, trimming hedges and pruning the many fruit trees. I discovered many new (to me anyway) recipes for pears!

We attended The International Church of Lund, which was associated with the Methodist Church and in July and August we provided the music for the services; me on piano, Ian on guitar and both of us singing. That gave me a focus during the week – to practice the hymns as I had never played piano for a congregation before. The first lesson Ian and I learned was to make sure that our music was in the same key....unless of course you want to sound like a 'Les Dawson special'!

The church was truly international and we made many friends there, Asian, American, German, Swedish. We also met an Iranian at the library and he has also become a good friend!

Ron and I kept in touch by telephone whilst I was in Sweden. Ian and I were delighted to be invited to his 90th birthday party which had been arranged for Saturday 13th September – his birthday is actually 14th

September. So, Ian and I flew to London on 12th September to be informed that Ron was in hospital. The home had given me the phone number of another cousin who lived in Sunningdale and I called her. We met up at Ron's nursing home and my sister Rowena took Ian and I to visit Ron. He was pleased to see me and Ian but it was obvious that he was in a great deal of pain. Ian and I flew back to Copenhagen on Monday 14th September.

Ron was released from hospital back to the home and we kept in touch. Then I heard that he was back in hospital and I flew back to see him. As Ian was working I had to fly by myself and Ian would join me at the weekend. Ian had arranged for a Wokingham taxi to collect me from Heathrow airport and take me straight to the hospital in Reading. I was in tears the whole journey and in total panic when I arrived at Heathrow. There were so many people and I couldn't find the taxi; I called the taxi firm and a man told me to turn around as he was standing behind me! He asked if I was alright and I explained the situation to him. As he was a Wokingham taxi driver, he knew Ron and said that he would get me to hospital as quickly as he could. I went to see Ron as soon as I was dropped off. He said that he never thought that he would see me again. I told him that I can be very determined when I want to be. Ian arrived the next night (a Thursday as I remember) and we both visited Ron. It was during that time that John, Rowena, Fiona and myself all met up again after 16 years. That again was another emotional experience; even more so when Fiona asked me why I hadn't wanted anything to do with her or Rowena and John. I was completely taken aback and asked her what she meant.

The following information is so very important to my account of Henry's treatment of me and I shall be forever indebted to Fiona for asking the question.

She told me that she phoned me at the house (not

knowing that I was in hospital) and Henry had told her that 'I didn't want anything to do with her and my other sister and brother.' I then told her that Henry had told me that John, Rowena and Fiona wanted nothing to do with me. Because of that lie we lost 16 years. That was a very cruel, but typical act from Henry. He tried to isolate me from all my family, he even tried to isolate me from my eldest son Paul but that didn't work. OK, so it took 16 years and my sister to ask a very brave question, but the truth finally came out.

Ron did seem to 'perk up' during that week; but he had his final wish, that we (myself, John, Rowena and Fiona) would all be together again; he got that wish and was happy.

I stayed in Reading for a week visiting Ron twice a day. Once back in Sweden my mobile never left my side. I was just waiting for the call. It came on Monday 2nd November at 8pm on my mobile. Rowena phoned me, I didn't get to my phone in time and had to call her back. Later that night I received a text message from Fiona:- "Dad passed on with me holding his hand. I told him how much you loved him. He is at peace with God now! Love Fiona xx"

His funeral was on Monday 9th November at 2.45pm. Ian and I flew to Manchester, stayed overnight and then picked up my son Paul and drove to Wokingham. Ian and I sang a version of 'The Lord's My Shepherd' – as a duet – it was the only way I could get through the service; I had to have something to focus on. Ron's coffin was at my left hand side as I sang. We drove back to The Peak District the next day and flew back to Sweden on 11th November.

Neither of us were happy in Sweden, Ian wasn't happy with the work he had been given and he offered to take redundancy when it was announced that another 450 staff had to go. His offer was rejected on the grounds that his work was necessary so he resigned and took early retirement. We then started making plans to leave Sweden; we had holidayed in a place called Nerja in Spain in August 2009 and decided to move there – we could not afford to live back in the UK. We also made arrangements to marry and our Methodist Minister agreed to marry us on 18th September 2010.

Ian and I moved to Nerja on 1st March 2010 where we stayed for 18 months. Our financial situation then changed very suddenly and we were able to buy a little cottage in a village called Benamocarra which is only a 30 minute drive from Nerja. We intend to stay here now– we love being here and are very happy together.

Issues and Complaints

It will be apparent from the above narrative that I have many issues and complaints relating to:

- Medical Services
- Social Services
- The Benefit System
- Police
- Members of Parliament
- Lawyers
- Courts

Medical Services

On many occasions I was taken into hospital, placed on the psychiatric ward and referred to psychiatrists for treatment. However, on no occasion did a psychiatrist discuss the cause of my condition, all any of them did was suppress my mental activity by prescribing a cocktail of drugs; these did not help. All the drugs did was mask reality and increase my body weight; my weight increased from around 8.5 - 9 stones to 13.5 - 14 stones! If the doctors had taken time with me and listened then they may have realised that I was not mentally ill, which is what Henry claimed on many occasions, but I was suffering from acute mental distress, caused by his behaviour. One of the nurses understood this very clearly when she said that in the majority of cases the wrong partner was being treated.

It would also be useful if all GP surgeries had contact details of Women's Aid Refuges. If I had known that there was one so close to me I would have gone there for help.

Too many people, who had a history of mental health problems, have died because their physical health concerns have been dismissed.

Psychiatrists need to have the time to listen to their clients and be able to identify what is mental illness and what is mental distress.

GP's also need to listen to their patients and take them seriously.

One of the psychiatrists said that I would benefit from Cognitive Behavioural Therapy (CBT), unfortunately this was not provided by the NHS and I would have had to seek private therapy at a cost of £50/hour. This was clearly out of the question. However when visiting the Job-centre, my consultant said he could arrange CBT sessions for me so that I could get back to work! How weird is that? He also asked me why I was struggling so much financially as he said I must be receiving Income Support. I told him that I didn't know anything about that so he helped me apply – I should have been in receipt of Income Support since I left Henry but no-one had informed me. I asked for it to be back dated but was refused – I was told that it was my fault I hadn't claimed!

Government departments need to be better co-ordinated to provide services; it is illogical that the NHS could not provide CBT but the Job-centre could.

The Benefit System

The system is far too complex. How can members of the public be expected to know which benefits they are entitled to? I have read that the Government has plans to overhaul the system. It would be a great help if, when a person finds they are in need of help from the system, that one person could explain all the benefits to which they are entitled and help them with the applications.

I also think that Job-centres should be better equipped

to cope with post-graduates. The default seems to be that you are only capable of stocking shelves in the local supermarket!

Another problem with my benefits arose, when I moved about a mile within the same village because my new house was in a different county! That meant that my housing benefit was stopped and I had to apply all over again. Income support and DLA were not affected. The housing benefit staff told me that I was living in a house too big for just one person. It was a mid terraced, 2 up, 2 down property! MP's can have second homes and furnish them on expenses – outrageous!

A simple solution to this would be to have allocated fully furnished and equipped apartments in London for when MP's need to be in the city. No need then for any expense claims to furnish vast mansions.

Social Services

The lack of care and concern from social services for the welfare of my children still sickens me – the officers involved were obviously frightened of Henry. His bullying tactics at the Children in Need meetings should have been challenged and should have raised alarm bells, but they did as little as they could to avoid upsetting him; fairness and justice were not on their agenda.

Henry treated the whole process with contempt and this was plain to see, but this behaviour was tolerated by Social Services. What power and control was it that he had over them?

Social Services should take control over their meetings and not allow an individual to treat them with contempt, or browbeat them into implementing that individual's wishes.

Police

I have many issues with the way I was treated by the police.

Police should be impartial and treat all members of the public equally - so why was it that whenever Henry rang the police they attended immediately and treated me very aggressively? Yet, whenever I called them they only paid lip service. For example, after Henry had phoned them the police broke into my house damaging the back door and causing a lot of damage; yet when I phoned them to check the safety of my children they just went to the house and because it was in darkness they didn't pursue the matter. I was treated with contempt by the police because Henry had told them that I was mentally ill and they believed him, why? What power and control was it that he had over them? My complaint against the police was not upheld as they said they were acting 'in order to preserve life'. I was given the option of having the officer concerned 'disciplined' or sent on a Domestic Violence awareness course; in a moment of weakness (or maybe Christianity) I asked that he be sent on the course. I realise now that I was wrong; I should have insisted that the officer be disciplined as an example to others.

The police must also realise that it is extremely intimidating for a woman, (on her own) to be confronted by a lone male police officer. I am sure that even then it was against all their protocols.

Police are meant to protect the public and not be prejudiced, they should investigate each case as reported.

Lone male police officers should NOT be sent round to a lone female.

Members of Parliament

On a number of occasions I wrote to Members of Parliament seeking their support for a fair hearing in the Children in Need meetings but they seem to be powerless, why are MP's unable to help? I was under the misapprehension that they were there to serve and protect the public – oh yes – just like the police and social services do!

One problem that I faced was that Henry lived with our children, in one constituency and I lived in a neighbouring constituency, this seemed to pose an insurmountable problem for both MPs; neither would interfere in the other's patch.

There must be a better way for MPs to work on cross border issues.

Lawyers

It was not made clear to me when I started divorce proceedings, that Legal Aid is only a loan and is not a grant. It was also not made clear to me that if I was on Legal Aid that I would have to accept whichever barrister was available at the time of a court hearing; I rarely saw the same barrister twice! This inconsistency in my legal representation cost me dearly. If I had known this beforehand then somehow or other I would have found the means to avoid Legal Aid; that would have put me more in control and avoided a barrister's lottery.

As legal aid is only a loan, why are people claiming legal aid treated differently than people who are paying privately? Consistency of legal representation is essential to secure justice.

There is a legal procedure called 'Ex-parte' which Henry used to get a court order giving him guardianship and custody of the children. He paid to go before a judge and told him that custody of the children must be given to him as I was a 'mentally ill alcoholic'. That was a total untruth but was never questioned by the judge. British justice! If I had known about this procedure, I would have applied to the court first, as I did not, I was from that moment always on the defensive; Henry had the children and I had to battle in the courts to get minimal access rights.

The working of ex-parte judgements should be amended, it seems that in the UK there is no time limit for the judgement. In the USA the judgement has to be reviewed after a certain time period otherwise the decision lapses, this is fairer and the UK should adopt the same procedure.

Courts

In the court hearings Henry was given a hard time, being cross-examined in great detail. He was accused by the judge of being very devious, when he would not explain where £50,000 had disappeared from his assets. He also would not explain how he could afford to keep two children and run the huge house on his declared income. Yet none of these issues were pursued and the court did not force Henry to answer these questions. Consequently, I received an unfair settlement and Henry's contempt of the court orders meant that I lost all contact with Ben and Gerry.

Why did the judge not pursue the unanswered questions?

Conclusion

People I know have come up with a few ideas about Henry and the reason for his influence over the authorities. The main one is that he must have been (and maybe still is) a member of the masons. This may sound crazy, but nothing else makes any sense. He had the police and social services and maybe even the judges, wrapped around his little finger, not that any of his fingers were little! His faith in the occult and ouiji boards and tarot cards is also a very unlikely possibility, but I don't believe in that black magic stuff anyway.

It seems to me that 'justice' in the UK (I can only report on that) depends on your social standing; the fact that I was (and still am) a very well qualified women was totally negated by the fact that I wrongly spent time on psychiatric wards – due to my ex-husbands treatment of me.

The authorities must wake up and stop looking for 'easy' options. Equations do not always work – especially when the 'input' is incorrect or misleading. Maybe I need to clarify this statement:- I mean that a mother who has spent time on a psychiatric ward does not equate to a threat or danger to her children. The only person I ever physically harmed was myself and I still have the scars on my wrist to prove it – the internal scars (caused by Henry) may have healed by now – I don't know – I have been unable to go for a smear test even though I know one must be due. The mental scars never go away. They may diminish somewhat, but there is not a day that goes by when I am not thinking about Ben and Gerry.

I will admit that I did not want to be pregnant with Gerry but that was only because of the way she had been conceived. You cannot begin to imagine my feelings of guilt now that I have not seen her for so many years. The main question going through my mind is:- is this divine justice? I didn't want to be pregnant and so now I haven't got her in my life.

It is also very interesting to note that, not long after Henry paid the settlement money as directed by the court, he suddenly had the money to have major improvements done on the house. Scaffolding surrounded the entire house for just under 2 years and all the window and doors were replaced along with barge boards and soffits. He must have therefore either won the lottery (which I doubt) or, suddenly remembered where he had put his savings.

My Hopes for the future

My main desire is to be reunited with Ben and Gerry. I still write to them via school – that will not be possible when they leave. I have also been sending them private messages via Facebook. They have never acknowledged receipt of the messages, letters or cards that I send. The school has at least kept me up to date with school reports so I have some idea of how they are. I still have the 2 photographs on my mobile that Gerry put on it, I have the mother's day present that she bought me in 2004 – a little white trinket case in the shape of a swan, I have the 2 pictures that she drew of me that same year – they are on the fridge door and I have the pink hair slide that she put on the artificial pink flower. These are items that I will never part with. I have nothing from Ben.

My other wishes are that authorities will take note of my suggestions and that the situation can improve for people (male or female) who find themselves in a similar scenario to mine.

My final words to all the authorities are that the most important thing is that they treat everyone with respect and check out the facts properly before making rash decisions and taking rash actions.

Appendix 1 - Post Traumatic Stress Disorder (PTSD)

PTSD is a common reaction to very stressful or traumatic events. A traumatic event is one where we can see that we or other people are in danger, some examples are given here:-

- serious road accidents
- military combat
- violent personal assault
- being taken hostage
- being a prisoner of war
- natural or man made disasters
- being diagnosed with a life-threatening illness

The cause of my own PTSD was Henry's treatment of me, I have described earlier in this book how I was affected.

Appendices 2, 3 and 4 explain the courses that I used.

Appendix 5 talks about Parental Alienation and how it is also a form of child abuse.

Appendix 6 is the account of my first stay on a psychiatric ward.

Appendix 2 - Assertiveness training from hospital

I have to say that the so called 'courses' given to me at the hospitals were not very effective but on one of them I did come away with the following 'Personal Bill of Rights':-

- I have the right to be treated with respect as an equal human being.
- I have the right to acknowledge my needs as being equal to those of others.
- I have the right to express my opinions, thoughts and feelings.
- I have the right to make mistakes.
- I have the right to choose not to take responsibility for other people.
- I have the right to be me without being dependent on the approval of others.

We also discussed 'Behaviour Types' shown here:-

HANDOUT C: Behaviour Types

DIRECT AGGRESSION

- WHAT YOU COULD DO WITH...
- IF I WERE YOU I'D DO IT THIS WAY
- GET OUT OF MY WAY
- I ALWAYS WIN
- I DON'T GIVE A X X X ABOUT YOU
- HOW DARE YOU

**BOSSY
ARROGANT
BULLDOZING
INTOLERANT
OPINIONATED
OVER-BEARING**

INDIRECT AGGRESSION

- DON'T WORRY I CAN MANAGE
- MARTYRDOM'S MY WAY OF LIFE
- OF COURSE I'M NOT ANGRY
- CAN'T YOU TAKE A JOKE
- THAT'S PRETTY GOOD FOR SOMEONE LIKE YOU
- I'LL BE ILL IF YOU BEHAVE LIKE THAT

**SARCASTIC
DECEIVING
AMBIGUOUS
INSINUATING
MANIPULATIVE
GUILT INDUCING**

PASSIVITY

- WHATEVER YOU WANT'S OK BY ME
- I'M WAITING FOR MY LIFE TO GET BETTER
- I'M REALLY SORRY
- I'M NOT IMPORTANT
- I MUSTN'T ROCK THE BOAT
- NOTHING GOES RIGHT FOR ME

**WAITING
MOANING
HELPLESS
SUBMISSIVE
INDECISIVE
APOLOGETIC**

ASSERTIVENESS

- I HAVE THE RIGHT TO BE ME, YOU HAVE THE RIGHT TO BE YOU
- MY LIFE IS MY RESPONSIBILITY
- I'M NOT PERFECT
- I'LL TAKE A RISK
- I FEEL...
- I'M OK YOU'RE OK

**DIRECT
HONEST
POSITIVE
ACCEPTING
RESPONSIBLE
SPONTANEOUS**

Appendix 3 - *The Freedom Programme*

I actually stumbled across this course, whilst browsing in The Central Library one Saturday with Ben and Gerry looking for information for their homework.

The Freedom Programme was described as a course for women who had been, or were living, in an abusive relationship. As I was desperate for any help I could get, I went along to see what it was all about.

The course was very structured, but for me the most important part was realising that there were other women in similar or even worse situations to mine.

Suddenly I was not alone and people believed me. Even then though I could not bring myself to tell anyone about the sexual abuse as I was still too ashamed.

The woman who had set up the course had done so by talking with male abusers of women. It all comes down to power and control – of one person to another – regardless of gender.

The first item during the first session was to define 'abuse'.

'The wrongful application of power by a person/s in a dominant position'.

There are, as I have outlined previously, many different aspects to abuse:- psychological, emotional, physical, sexual and also financial.

The charts of Power and Control are included here:-

Lynne Hanson

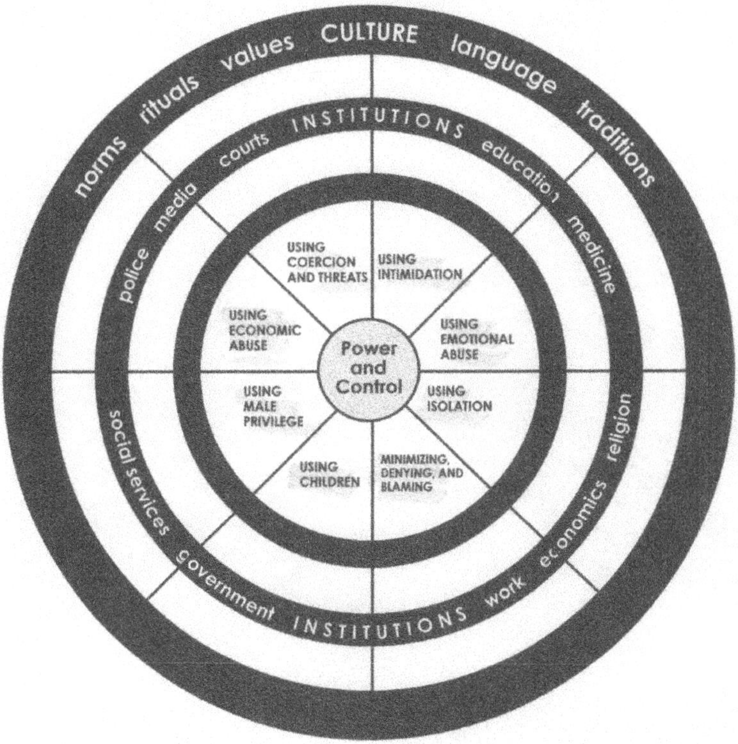

Escaping The Fear

POWER AND CONTROL WHEEL

Physical and sexual assaults, or threats to commit them, are the most apparent forms of domestic violence and are usually the actions that allow others to become aware of the problem. However, regular use of other abusive behaviors by the batterer, when reinforced by one or more acts of physical violence, make up a larger system of abuse. Although physical assaults may occur only once or occasionally, they instill threat of future violent attacks and allow the abuser to take control of the woman's life and circumstances.

The Power & Control diagram is a particularly helpful tool in understanding the overall pattern of abusive and violent behaviors, which are used by a batterer to establish and maintain control over his partner. Very often, one or more violent incidents are accompanied by an array of these other types of abuse. They are less easily identified, yet firmly establish a pattern of intimidation and control in the relationship.

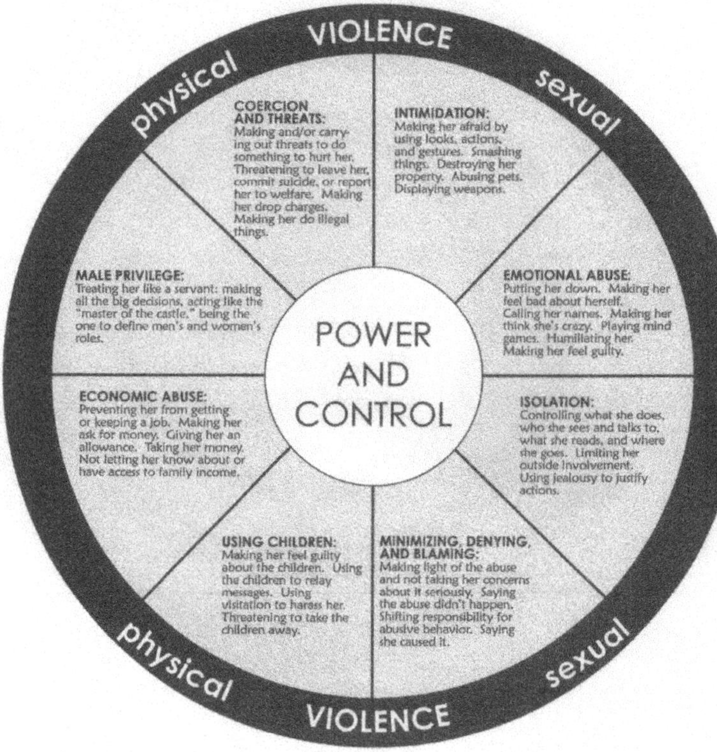

VIOLENCE physical sexual

COERCION AND THREATS: Making and/or carrying out threats to do something to hurt her. Threatening to leave her, commit suicide, or report her to welfare. Making her drop charges. Making her do illegal things.

INTIMIDATION: Making her afraid by using looks, actions, and gestures. Smashing things. Destroying her property. Abusing pets. Displaying weapons.

MALE PRIVILEGE: Treating her like a servant: making all the big decisions, acting like the "master of the castle," being the one to define men's and women's roles.

EMOTIONAL ABUSE: Putting her down. Making her feel bad about herself. Calling her names. Making her think she's crazy. Playing mind games. Humiliating her. Making her feel guilty.

ECONOMIC ABUSE: Preventing her from getting or keeping a job. Making her ask for money. Giving her an allowance. Taking her money. Not letting her know about or have access to family income.

ISOLATION: Controlling what she does, who she sees and talks to, what she reads, and where she goes. Limiting her outside involvement. Using jealousy to justify actions.

USING CHILDREN: Making her feel guilty about the children. Using the children to relay messages. Using visitation to harass her. Threatening to take the children away.

MINIMIZING, DENYING, AND BLAMING: Making light of the abuse and not taking her concerns about it seriously. Saying the abuse didn't happen. Shifting responsibility for abusive behavior. Saying she caused it.

POWER AND CONTROL

VIOLENCE physical sexual

Developed by:
Domestic Abuse Intervention Project
202 East Superior Street
Duluth, MN 55802
218.722.4134

Produced and distributed by:

NATIONAL CENTER
on Domestic and Sexual Violence
training · consulting · advocacy

7800 Shoal Creek, Ste 120-N · Austin, Texas 78757
tel: 512.407.9020 · fax 512.407.9022 · www.ncdsv.org

Each week the course looked at different aspects of 'The Dominator':- that chart is shown here:-

Escaping The Fear

The 8 aspects of that 'character' were then discussed each week until we finally arrived at 'Mr Right' included here:-

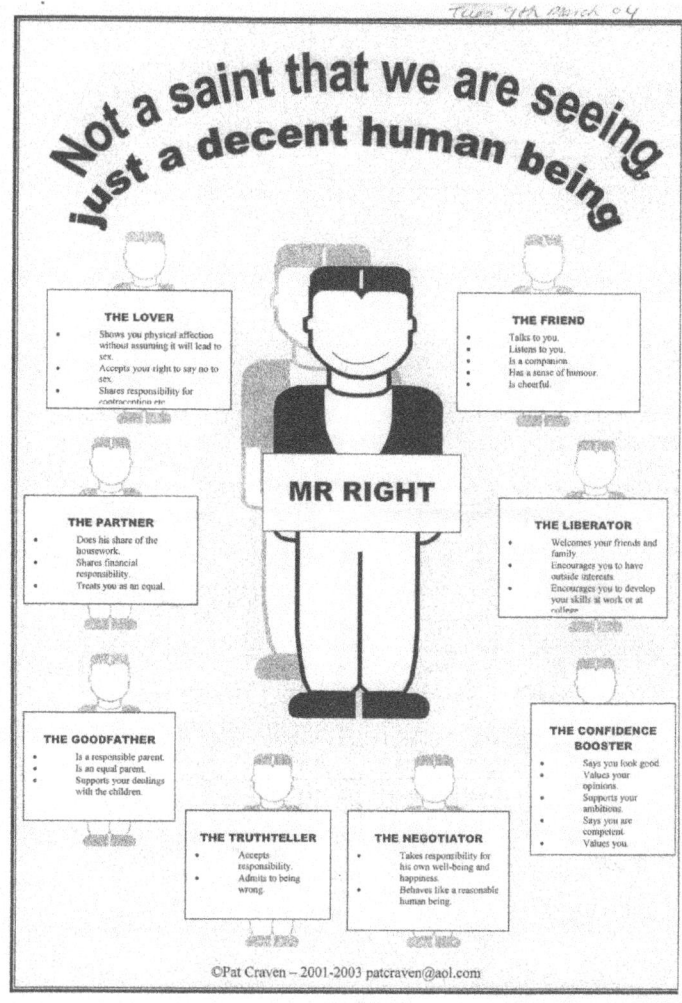

Another aspect covered was 'Children Coping with Family Violence'.

We also covered 'The Rules of the Game'; these were very important to Henry who wanted to control everything and treat me as his property.

The next step was to look at how men should behave towards their partners/wives and how an ideal family life should be.

The final session was about 'Warning Signs' – perhaps this list should be given out to every girl on leaving school! Here it is:-

WARNING SIGNS

Examples of Warning signs

If we visit a friend and he insists on dropping us off and collecting us. He *may* genuinely be trying to protect us from the elements or he *may* be making sure we are where we say we will be and there are no men there.

He moves in with us too soon.

He comes on too strong, wanting to see us every day.

He telephones all the time.

He buys us a mobile phone to "make sure we are safe".

Asks where we have been and who with.

Calls round late at night unannounced.

Uses phrases like "together for life," and "always".

Doesn't want to socialise with our friends.

Insists on buying clothes or shopping.

Criticises his former partners.

Does not use our name. Calls us "love" or "babe" or refers to us as his "bird"

May be moody but won't explain why.

Puts us down in front of others but always uses humour to do it.

Starts doing our DIY as soon as he meets us. Before we know it Dado rails have sprung up all over the house. He can then come round and rip them down if we try to end the relationship.

Tries to persuade us not to go to work.

Tries to monopolise our time.

Stands us up or arrives late.

Makes racist or sexist jokes

We feel uneasy but ignore it

More information about The Freedom Programme can be found on their website:
http://www.freedomprogramme.co.uk/index.php

Appendix 4 - Cognitive Behavioural Therapy (CBT)

The most important requirement is that you find a therapist who you trust and feel comfortable with. I was extremely lucky as the lady who been assigned to me was wonderful. As I mentioned, the first task is retelling your story.

My first 'assignment':-

Please write at least one page on what it means to you that you were in this relationship (with Henry). Consider the effects this had on your beliefs about yourself, your beliefs about others, and your beliefs about the world. Also consider the following topics while writing your answer: safety, trust, power/competence, esteem and intimacy.

Bring this with you to the next session.

That task was not too difficult to do – though it did take me some time to get it in a sensible format that would be easily read.

The next task was very hard to do:-

Write a detailed account of the traumatic event, include as many sensory details as possible. Also includes thoughts and feelings about how you felt during the event.

If you are unable to write it in one sitting, draw a line and continue on at the point you remember next. Re-read the account to yourself everyday until the next session.

The purpose of this assignment is to enable you to get the full memory back, for you to feel the emotions about it, and for you and I to begin to look for 'stuck' points.

I did eventually manage to write that account but I had to break off four times and then start again. That was taken to my next session and we read through it together and discussed it at length. My next task was:-

Write out the entire account again. Add any details that might have been left out of the first account, as well as to record any thoughts and feelings you are having now in parentheses, along with your thoughts and feelings at the time.

Read through the account everyday, preferably early evening so that you can dream about it, exposure should last between 45 minutes to one hour/day.

That assignment took up 3 sides of A4 paper and I broke off writing once to be sick.

There was another assignment alongside that one; it was to keep a record of how 'anxious' I felt whilst reading the account. I had to give a rating (out of 10) and also write a comment. I read my account 8 times with 4 different people and only managed to get my 'anxiety rating' down from 10 to 8.

A similar exercise was applied to 'trauma triggers'. The trigger (e.g. 'sudden noises') was written in 1 column along with how often that occurred , the next column was to describe the memory/sensation. Another column asked if the trigger could be avoided and the final column was for a 'distress rating': 0-10.

I filled in 2.5 sheets of A4!

There were just 2 more exercise sheets to fill in – over many weeks though.

I had to write down an 'activating event', what I believed about it and what I did as a result. I completed six of those sheets and have included just one here.

Lynne Hanson

Date: ....

Activating Event	Belief	Consequence
A →	B →	→ C
"Something happens"	"I tell myself something"	"I feel and do something"
The phone rings. I am forbidden to answer the 'phone. I hear a loud noise - He would hammer on the window	He is checking up on me. Reminds me Pete coming home	Utter panic sets in. My heart races & I don't know what to do. as above - I think I'm going to be in trouble - I always was when he came home. People find it amusing when I react as I do & then feel even worse

Does it make sense to tell yourself the above?...
....
What can you tell yourself on such occasions in the future?..
....

The next task was then to look at each of those sheets and examine my thinking and my resultant behaviour. This was then applied to other 'events' and proved to be a very interesting exercise for myself and Ian to do together.

It takes a great deal of work and commitment to get through a CBT course but I was determined to try to get back to being 'me'.

A useful link for more information about CBT is from the British Association for Behavioural and Cognitive Psychotherapies: www.babcp.com

Appendix 5 - Parental Alienation

Parental Alienation is a very well documented phenomenon but unfortunately rarely hits the headlines. This is what so many parents (of either sex) resort to and I am unsure of the reasoning behind it. In my case it was certainly because Henry was (and is) very insecure and very possessive. He was a like a toddler – if the object is not pinned down, then it is his!

I found many references to Parental Alienation on the internet and have given quotes from 3 of them here.

The first is taken from "How to Cope with the Effects of Parental Alienation" by Dr Reena Sommer, Ph.D.

Early signs of Parental Alienation.

Children perceive you as causing financial problems of the other parent.

Children appear to have knowledge of details relating to the legal aspects of the divorce.

Children show sudden negative change in their attitude toward you.

Children are uncharacteristically rude and /or belligerent to you.

Access time is not occurring as agreed upon by court orders and visitation is cut back by the other parent.

The ex-husband/wife/partner undermines you in front of the children.

The ex-husband/wife/partner refers to you as being abusive and a risk to the children.

These are just a few of the things that I have had to cope with.

The New York Law Journal published an article written by Joel R Brandes on March 26th 2000, entitled

"Parental Alienation". The important paragraph is this:-

'We believe that inducing parental alienation in a child is a form of child abuse, which should be punishable as abuse under the Family Court Act. Moreover, a parent who alienates a child against the other parent should be denied visitation with all of his /her children until the child is no longer alienated against the target parent.'

Another article :- "The Judiciary's Role in the Etiology, Symptom Development and Treatment of the Parental Alienation Syndrome (PAS)" written by Richard A. Gardner, MD says:-

The alienating parent's primary purpose for indoctrinating into the children a campaign of denigration against the target parent is to gain leverage in court. The child's alienation has less to do with bona fida animosity or even hatred of the alienated parent, but more to do with the fear that if such acrimony is not exhibited, the alienating parent will reject the child.

I am not entirely in agreement with that thought; I had been hurt mentally and physically by Henry, so the only way he could inflict any more hurt was by alienating our children and isolating them from me. Unfortunately with the assistance of the courts he succeeded in this.

APPENDIX 6

RECORD OF DAYS SPENT ON THE PSYCHIATRIC WARD

DAY 1   20 December 1995 (Wednesday)

Arrived 1 hour late at 11.30 am due to Henry having a doctor's appointment for his continuing dizzy spells. A nurse took some brief details when she had shown me my bed and then we (Henry, myself and the babies) went to the canteen for some lunch. I shared a bowl of soup with Gerry and a pudding with Henry, Ben and Gerry. I then walked back to the car with Henry to help him get the babies in the car and came back to my bed to wait for the doctor who was due to see me at 12.50 pm.

I had a long wait in what was called the "quiet room" and was asked to leave by people wanting to hold a meeting. When the doctor arrived we went into the room next door labelled the "beauty room". The doctor explained that she was a registrar and wanted to hear the background to my case. That meant that I had to give a potted history of my life - not a fun story - after which she asked about sleep, libido and appetite. The whole session must have lasted at least an hour, maybe one hour and a half. I felt that I'd been put through the mill again. After the session she gave me a very quick medical and then I went to the canteen again and had a sandwich and some diet coke to get some change for the phone. I phoned Jo (a girl friend who lived near me) and then had to express as much milk as I could as I was so uncomfortable with not feeding Gerry.

The tea arrived about 5pm or 5.30pm I think and I had the fish - it was awful, very dry and full of bones. I felt very agitated and all worked up. I phoned Henry at around 7pm as I thought it would be quiet at home by then, but he was giving the babies their tea and wanted me to phone back later - I had put a £1 coin in though so I only used up 50p worth.

He is quite angry that I have come into hospital now - "Why didn't you tell me 2 weeks ago?" He knows I wanted to come in back in September when it was suggested. I couldn't because of Henry's courses - they didn't all run in the end anyway, so I think I should have come in then and I might have been better by now.

The drain is going to be unblocked at 12.30pm tomorrow, Thursday and Henry is counselling in the morning. Paul is coming to look after the babies. I don't know what will happen when Henry's classes start up again on 8th January 1996. A social worker is supposed to be getting in touch with him - not that they do any good.

I felt really wound up and guilty about being in here and my mind is full of all sorts - I was washing up the pots and cleaning the kitchen around midnight - I was given an extra sleeping tablet and went back to bed but still couldn't settle and became very upset. I sat and talked to a nurse called Jean (I think) and managed to sleep between 2 and 5am.

Day 2 - 21 December 1995

The lights were switched on about 7.30am, I think, just when you could carry on sleeping. I got up about 8am and made myself a cup of tea and carried on with my knitting. I had some porridge and a roll for breakfast and a cup of coffee but the tea and coffee all taste sweet somehow and I can't stand that. I carried on knitting and finished one sleeve. By then it was 10.30am and I went for a shower. I was given some medication as I felt all wound up and all shaky.

I spent most of the day knitting and then had a sleep and at 5pm one of the nurses, woke me to say that Henry had phoned and I was to call him back. He was supposed to be coming to visit me but on the 'phone he said he will come tomorrow afternoon.

I still feel really awful. I was also promised some medication to stop my milk because I am very uncomfortable but all they gave me was two paracetamol tablets.

I phoned Pete, a friend and work colleague, and asked if he would visit me sometime and he said he would.

At 10pm I asked for the medication they had promised to take my milk away, but they didn't know anything about it and just gave me two paracetamol again. I took two sleeping tablets as well as the anti-depressants (chlorpromisine) as I desperately wanted a good night's sleep.

Day 3 22nd December 1995 (Friday)

I woke up at 6am (a good night's sleep for me) and could hear the wind howling through the windows. (My bed is at the end of the ward next to the windows.) I had had another weird dream. A little boy (Paul or Ben) was giving a talk on a sort of documentary programme for TV, about some new housing development of the future in which all the houses/flats were the same, all crowded on top of each other, with space for a car and then lots of steps down to the front door. Then I was in the living room at home and my mother was there looking after a little boy who had Down's Syndrome and his surname was Armstrong-Jones. Then I was outside the house with Ben and found a present for him left at the front door by the steps but I couldn't get down the step with him, so I walked round to the driveway front door and went in to see my Mum. I don't know why I should dream about my Mum, but she was certainly much nicer in my dream than she was in real life.

After my porridge I had a shower and went to the confidence building course.

I feel so drained, weary, worn out and fed-up and if I have to sit at the dining table with one of the male patients again I'll be sick I'm sure. His nose is always running and he is constantly sniffing and doesn't like having baths.

The rest of the day was taken up with knitting. I want to have Henry's jumper finished for him for Christmas. I have been given 3 different stories about what to do about the breast milk. I was getting quite uncomfortable:-
1) express the milk frequently or else I'd get blocked ducts and possibly mastitis.
2) I would be given some medication to stop the milk being produced.
3) Just to leave things alone, suffer the pain for a few days and the milk will stop.

Henry visited me with the babies around tea time but the canteen was closed and so we went to the WRVS lounge to talk, but Ben was such a pest we couldn't really talk and the visit was a disaster. When they left I went back for my tea but it had gone so all I managed to get was a sandwich (egg salad). All I had eaten was a bowl of porridge at breakfast as the dinner was dried up fish bone which was inedible.

I was quite upset after Henry's visit as Ben wouldn't kiss me good bye and Henry had the nerve to ask me to phone up for an Indian take away for him!

About 9pm I put my knitting away and walked out of the hospital. I was hoping to fall under a passing car (or bus). However, I just wandered about outside and couldn't get to the road from where I was. I found a door back into the hospital (by the coronary care ward) and walked to the main entrance and kept going in and out. Eventually, further down the corridor I found the Chapel. This is open 24 hours a day, so I went in. There was an upright piano in one corner so I went to play it. I haven't played the piano for about 16 years and I could hardly even play a scale. I stayed in the Chapel for some time and then walked back to the ward. It is ten past ten and the tablets were being given out. I collected mine and was very upset. One of the nurses had a chat to me and I went to bed after phoning Henry.

Day 4 23rd December 1995 (Saturday)

I just didn't want to get up today, I felt so miserable but I got up at 10am and had a bowl of cornflakes. Several people were going home today for Christmas. I am going home tomorrow and returning on Wednesday.

I spent the day knitting and finished the other sleeve. Henry came just after 1pm so I had already had a sandwich. We all went down to the canteen. Gerry ate beans, chips, quiche, apple crumble and custard and half a Milky Way. Ben ate a little but was more interested in playing with a balloon he had found on the Christmas tree.

It was a much better visit today but he still wouldn't kiss me goodbye - he wanted me to get into the car in the front seat. Henry had brought in the rest of the jumper but no darning needle. One of the nurses found one for me. I got into trouble for having a pair of scissors on the bed. They were only little blunt ended scissors out of a handbag first aid kit. Anyway, they had to be locked away and I was to ask for them when I needed them.

I sat up until 10.30pm to finish all the knitting. I had my tablets and then phoned Henry. I was quite worried about going to bed, as during the afternoon the police brought in a thalidomide man who was very abusive to the staff. He had another go at the staff later and they sent for two men who gave him an injection. If he wasn't so nasty, it could have been quite funny. He was looking for John Major, and said Sky TV were going to ring him. When he heard his name on TV he blew up, saying that they were infringing copyright by using his name without permission. Then he started on about the police - he kept asking if they were a company and could he get shares in them. I was quite relieved when he went to bed, but also nervous as his bedroom was very near my ward, and there is no door on the ward. The night staff said that he had taken off his wooden leg. It still took me a while to get to sleep and I got up in the night at 3am.

Day 5 - 24th December 1995 (Sunday)

I woke up at about 6.45am and I thought I'd better start doing the jumper straight away. I had to get it finished before midday when Henry is coming to collect me.

I finished the jumper at about 10.30am and then went to have a shower. I'm now just waiting for Henry. He was due at noon but was one hour late. The first thing he told me was that the South African trip was off. We had planned to go over after Easter next year and visit his cousin and my brother. However, his cousin, had told him to cancel as she thought it was too dangerous with all the car jackings.

We went for a final shopping trip to Asda and went for a

drink in McDonalds. Tea was just a curry from Asda. Henry had some beer and I had the white wine that was left in the box. When the babies had gone to bed I got all the presents off the top of my wardrobe and put them round the tree. Andrea and Jeanette called round with a present for Ben and Gerry, they had a drink (sherry for Andrea) and a look at the wardrobe in the garage. It was exactly the same as the one they had already.

Day 6 – Monday 25th December 1995

We all got up and had some breakfast – I kept Ben in the kitchen with me while Henry took some 'photos of the Christmas tree with the presents around it. After breakfast we went into the living room and began to open the presents. We took a lot of photographs. Ben became very excited.

While the babies were playing in the front room Henry and I went into the kitchen to start the dinner and we opened a bottle of Cava to drink while preparing the vegetables. Henry went up to bed when the dinner was in the oven. He got up around 6pm, I think, and we had the meal in the dining room, with a bottle of red wine. I made up a 'special' bottle of red wine for Ben and Gerry, apple juice (sparkling) mixed with diluted apple and blackberry juice served in an old red wine bottle. Ben was quite happy with that as he thought he was having his own bottle of wine.

Later that evening Gerry needed a clean nappy so I started to change her downstairs. Henry went mad and went up to his room. About half an hour later he came down and I was changing Ben. So he went mad again and went back upstairs. I was quite upset (I can never seem to do anything right for him). I got Gerry to bed and Ben and I watched the film 'Sister Act' with Whoopi Goldberg. When Ben and I came up to bed, Henry was sat in his bedroom reading. I was upset and annoyed that he wouldn't spend the evening with me as I was only home until Wednesday.

I thought that I had better make sure I was out of the way tomorrow, so I took all the tablets the hospital had given me (12) to make sure that I slept all the next day. When he came into my room I told him what I had done – he just said that he was fed-up with these overdoses and that I should do it properly.

Day 7 Tuesday 26th December 1995

I just stayed in bed all day and all night: I got up once at 9.30am to answer the phone – it was my Dad (I had phoned John on Christmas day while Henry was asleep in the afternoon). His advice is to go over. I got up later to change Ben's nappy – he stayed with me most of the day.

Day 8 – Wednesday 27th December 1995

We all got up about 10am and had a breakfast of the cooked bacon and turkey sausage. I sorted out the washing. The kitchen sink was blocked by frozen water in the pipe outside, so I had to wash the pots in the butler's sink in the laundry room.

When we were all bathed and dressed we went out. Henry called at a bank and then called at a bookshop as it had a 25% off sale. When he got back to the car Henry asked if I wanted to go back home as it was just after 3.30pm. I said yes – I wanted to have a nice last meal with him before going back to the hospital.

We got the tea sorted as soon as we got in – I set the dining table again and the babies really liked the turkey again. We never got round to having any Christmas cake though and Henry went up to bed. I watched Star Trek and about 7pm I went to wake Henry as I had to get back to the hospital. Just as were leaving, the phone rang – it was the hospital checking when I was returning.

When I got back to the hospital I said a quick goodbye to Henry – kissed Gerry but Ben wouldn't kiss me goodbye. I sorted myself out and went straight to bed. I was woken at 10.30pm to have my tablets. I was still upset by Henry because he told me off for not clearing the dining table, even though I'd washed up a stack of dishes and sorted the washing out for him.

Day 9 – Thursday 28th December 1995

I got up at 8.30am (I'd had a good night's sleep thanks to the tablets) and ate some porridge and a roll and marmalade. Then I went back to bed I felt so awful. I went for a shower at 11.30am after another patient suggested that I might feel better. That patient came with me to the dining room for our lunch – mine was a ham salad – again. After lunch (about 1.30pm) I had a message to phone Henry.

The phone call was upsetting. I'm sure he doesn't understand why I am in here. One of the nurses came to me and I told her what had happened Christmas night, she got a senior nurse to come and talk to me who said that I would have to see the Doctor again.

I phoned a friend and colleague from BNFL, in the evening and they said they would visit me. Today was just another horrible day to get through.

Day 10 – Friday 29th December 1995

I got dressed straight away this morning as I didn't feel

like messing with a shower. I started knitting the jacket for Gerry. About 3.30pm I went for a shower and Henry arrived before I had finished. When I was ready we went down to the canteen to get Ben and Gerry some tea. Some progress had been made with the social services about my incapacity benefit and child care arrangements.

The doctor saw me this afternoon and I have decided not to go home at the weekend. I don't want to be in trouble again.

Just as Henry was leaving, a couple of friends arrived so they came with me while I ate my tea – another salad.

In the evening I phoned another friend and Paul but he was out.

Day 11 – Saturday 30 December 1995
Day 12 – Sunday 31 December 1995
Day 13 – Monday 1 January 1996
Not much to report for these days, - just knitting, eating, reading and sleeping

Day 14 – Tuesday 2nd January 1996

Today was not a good day. I was very jittery and jumpy, maybe because I would be seeing the doctor in the afternoon. I had cancelled my meeting with the counsellor.

Henry arrived about 3.30pm and shortly after a large man told me to go in to see the doctor. This doctor had one of the nurses with him in the room along with another man and woman. I didn't know them. Henry went out with the babies and they started asking me questions but I couldn't cope with all of them so I ran out when Henry came in. I had to have some more tablets to calm myself down. I went to bed early and I had to be woken to take my tablets at 10pm.

Day 15 – Wednesday 3rd January 1996

I was very tired and didn't get up until 11.45am when one of the nurses made me. I was just worn out after yesterday.

Today is the first day that the babies have been with the child-minder. I phoned Henry and he said that they had settled in O.K.

Joe came to visit me just after lunch and then I went to Relaxation. When I returned to the ward I found that I had missed my friend and colleague from BNFL.

Henry and the babies arrived while I was eating my tea.

Day 16 – Thursday 4th January 1996

Today I am having a day out in Manchester with Henry. He picked me up about 9.15am and we went straight to the shops. We started off in Waterstones and found the Mahler album he wanted straight away. We then went to look in Dillons but they didn't have anything. We then went to buy my vanity case from Argos and then had lunch in China town – a special Dim Sum lunch. Then it was back to Boots to collect the family planning video, baby wipes etc and onto the bookshop where Henry bought a book on Blake and I bought him the Mahler album we found earlier. We had a coffee and hot chocolate in The Opera Café and he then took me back to the hospital and he went on to collect the babies.

Day 17 – Friday 5th January 1996

I was up early today so that I could get some porridge and be ready for my course. This week we did 'How to Receive Criticism'.

Henry came after tea and we went to Asda shopping. Ben is not well at all and I asked the nurse in charge if he would let me go home for the weekend. He agreed as long as I came back on Saturday to take my tablets.

When we got home I couldn't believe the state of the house, papers (supposedly sorted) all over the carpet in the living room and both sinks overflowing with dirty pots.

Day 18 –Saturday 6th January 1996

I thought that I had better start to tackle the pots this morning and try to get them out of the way before Paul arrived. He was 1 hour late as he missed his train so he didn't come until 12.30pm. He had bought presents for the babies (books) and chocolate for me and Henry. Henry went back to bed in the afternoon and I sorted out the washing and finished the rest of the pots. When Henry got up he took Paul over to his Gran's.

Ben had another very disturbed night – high temperature and drinking lots of water, so I didn't sleep well again.

Day 19 – Sunday 7th January 1996

Today we tidied up the living room and put the Christmas tree away. Henry sorted through all the papers he had scattered over the floor. I went to the shops for his newspapers and to get some pads as my period had started last night.

We got a roast chicken dinner ready for later. I woke

Henry at 5.15pm and we ate about 6pm but the chicken wasn't done through properly. Then Henry took me back to the hospital.

I went to bed and had to be woken at 10.30pm to take my tablets.

Day 20 – Monday 8th January 1996

I got up at 8.45am, too late to go to the canteen for breakfast so I had a shower, washed my hair and ate a couple of brown rolls.

While I was sat trying to read, a lady from O.T. came to talk to me and has given me a programme with something every day.

After lunch, another salad, the doctor came to see me about changing my tablets from Chlorpromisine to Prozac, as she said that I hadn't made any progress. I thought that I was getting better so I felt very depressed and anxious about the change. She said that I should see a psychologist, when I'm discharged, as an outpatient.

I phoned home in the evening to see how the babysitter was getting on. Ben was asleep on the settee and Gerry was asleep in her cot.

I was very anxious and had to wait until 10pm for the tablets so that I could have the little white tablets to help me sleep.

Day 21 – Tuesday 9th January 1996

I was up early and showered and had breakfast at 8.30am as I had to go off to craft in O.T. At 9.30am. I took my knitting along – the cardigan for Gerry - but I couldn't concentrate and kept making mistakes as the room was full of people and a radio was playing.

After dinner I tried to have a sleep until Henry arrived. We had to wait until 3.30pm to see a different doctor. I had to go in on my own at first. The room was full of people again and I felt terrible. They decided to increase the dose of my tablets rather than change them and have agreed to let me have a day out on Sunday as long as I promise not to do any housework. They said that I set myself too difficult tasks and that I'm a perfectionist. I don't quite believe that though. Then Henry went in on his own and we discussed what happened over a cup of tea in the canteen.

I went to bed at 7.30pm after having a bath and was woken up at 10pm to take my tablets, except they hadn't got them and I was waiting until 1.30am.

Day 22 – Wednesday 10th January 1996

I did not want to get up this morning due to taking the tablets so late last night. However, I had to tell the nurses 3 times to leave me alone and I got up at 9.45am and had a shower and then another sleep. I felt really awful, I don't feel that I'm getting any better at all – no body seems to get better here, they just keep coming back or stay for weeks, months and even years.

I had lunch and then another sleep. At 1.30pm I had to go to Pottery – I didn't really want to go and in fact I only stayed for five minutes. I felt like a fish out of water; it just wasn't me at all. So I left and went back to bed until tea time and then went straight back to bed. One of the patients woke me at 9pm as my friend from work was on the phone for me. I told him that I didn't really feel very good at all.

When the night staff gave out the tablets I put mine under my tongue and just pretended to take them. I thought of saving all up until I had enough to do some damage. I really didn't feel like facing the world any more.

Day 23 – Thursday 11th January 1996

I had a shower quite early (7.30am) and then gave the tablets to the nurse who took me immediately to see the nurse in charge. He did his best to reassure me that people do get better but it just takes time – too much time if you ask me. I've been on anti-depressants since July and in here for three weeks.

I went to the relaxation with another patient at 1.30pm. When we came back she had been moved to a dormitory at the back to make room for a new lady opposite me. She is not happy about that and neither am I.

This time I took the tablets as I wanted to sleep but I still felt awful.

Day 24 – Friday 12th January 1996

I missed breakfast so I just had a bread roll on the ward. I was expecting to see Henry and the babies at lunch time and to go out with them. However, I phoned him at 1, 2 and 3pm with no answer so I thought he was out somewhere else. At 3.45pm I was asked to phone Henry. He had gone to bed at 12.45pm and only just woken up and that he was thinking of not coming to see me. I was so upset at this that I just put the phone down and went back to bed. I was woken up by Henry at my bedside but I was too upset to talk to him and he went away again. I then tried to phone him several times but didn't get to speak to him until much later that night. He had been to visit one of his friends and eaten fish and chips in the car. We talked a little and he asked me to phone him in the morning.

Day 25 – Saturday 13th January 1996

I did as I was told and phoned Henry early on (just after my breakfast – a bowl of porridge). He said that he had a lot to do as some of his friends were due to arrive at 5pm and he didn't know if he would have time to visit me. I told him it was up to him and what his priorities were. Anyway, he arrived at 10.30am (I was back in bed still feeling awful). We got the babies out of the car and went to the canteen. Henry had a bacon roll and the babies had Weetabix, scones, apples, milky ways, and then back on the ward, Gerry had a bread roll and Gwen's fruit salad and cream.

While we were talking I asked if I could come home today – the staff agreed but it took 1 hour to get my tablets. That meant that I could help Henry tidy up and get ready for his friends. I washed up and we prepared the tea together – one of the pies we had made earlier (chicken and wood pigeon). They arrived on time and we ate straight away. Our visitors washed up for me and then Henry and his friend went off to the concert. I gave Ben and Gerry a bath while my friend tried to fix the tiles in the shower. She also fixed the door rim. When both babies were in their pyjamas we went down to watch 'Casualty' and had a glass of wine. We put the babies to bed at 9pm.

Henry phoned at 10pm to say they would be on the last train and would arrive at 11.30pm. I phoned for a curry at 11pm and went to pick that up. It was about 1am when our friends left and I was very tired.

Day 26 – Sunday 14th January 1996

I did not have a good night's sleep as Ben came in with me. When he was settled I went into his room.

We were all up at 8.30am and Henry made bacon and mushrooms and tomatoes for our breakfast. Paul came around 1.45pm, just as Henry had gone back to bed. I sorted out the washing and ironed the babies clothes. Henry got up at 5pm and gave Paul a lift home. I was disappointed that Henry had been in bed for so long as we were going to try and sort out our holiday for after Easter. We had to leave at 7.30pm to get me back to the hospital.

It's quite depressing being back – I just want to stay at home now. Henry says I must stay until I'm better – he doesn't know how I feel though.

Day 27 – Monday 15th January 1996

I slept well and was up and showered by 8.30am so I could get my porridge and go to craft.

Henry had given me one of his jumpers to mend so I did that in craft and then started on making some little toy bags for the babies.

After lunch I looked through the holiday brochures for cottages in France and worked out ferry routes and fares (as requested by Henry). He came after tea with the babies – but they were both very tired and Ben was crying nearly all the time.

I tried to talk to Henry about the holiday – I thought we were going at the end of March/ beginning of April as soon as his courses had finished but of course that was all wrong – he said it would be too cold! So I had to go through the brochures again and work out for May.

Day 28 – Tuesday 16th January 1996

In craft, I finished one toy bag, started another and mended another jumper for Henry. I can't do any knitting in craft as it's too noisy.

A doctor came to see me during my break from craft and we had a chat. I told her that I was fine this week (last week was awful) and she said that I had 'turned the corner' and that I must think of the babies as they need me. In the ward round another doctor said that I can go home on Friday for the weekend (back on Sunday evening)

Day 29 – Wednesday 17th January 1996

Henry arrived at 1pm to take me out to lunch.

I got back on the ward about 3pm and slept until 5pm.

I have no idea why I stopped writing at that point.

Escaping The Fear

www.ingramcontent.com/pod-product-compliance
Lightning Source LLC
Chambersburg PA
CBHW022132080426
42734CB00006B/332